How to Fight a Data Center

A Citizen's Guide to Data Center Deals

Michael J Bommarito II

2026

The information in this book is intended for educational purposes only and does not constitute legal, financial, or professional advice. Readers should consult qualified professionals regarding their specific circumstances.

Published in the United States of America.

ISBN 979-8-9947460-8-0 (paperback)
ISBN 979-8-9947460-7-3 (ebook)

Cover image based on *John L. Sullivan, Champion Pugilist of the World* by E. W. Kemble, Wm. M. Clarke, 1883. Library of Congress.

First Edition, February 2026

Publisher's Cataloging-in-Publication Data
Names: Bommarito, Michael J., II, author.
Title: How to fight a data center :
    a citizen's guide to data center deals / Michael J Bommarito II.
Description: First edition. | Michigan : 2026.
Identifiers: ISBN 979-8-9947460-8-0 (paperback) | ISBN 979-8-9947460-7-3 (ebook)
Subjects: LCSH:
    Data centers—United States—Citizen participation.
    Data centers—Law and legislation—United States.
    Land use—United States—Planning.
    Community development—United States.
    Electric utilities—United States.

Classification: LCC TK5105.85 .B662 2026 | DDC 004.6—dc23

Contents

Introduction

"Move fast and break things" was a motto for building software. But this is not software. This is your water, your land, your jobs, your community. The things they break do not get patched in the next release.

More than $1 trillion in data center investment is reshaping America. More than six hundred projects are underway across all fifty states, and the power grid is straining to keep up. In community after community, the pattern is the same: the deal gets done before residents know it exists. The hearing happens after the outcome is decided. The promises come from people who will not be around to keep them.

That is not just bad policy. It breaks the social contract between the people who profit from a place and the people who live there.

I believe that destroying public trust in this technology is a bigger threat to American prosperity than anything China or Russia can do. Ramming it through communities that never agreed to bear the costs is the fastest way to lose that trust. And a country that fractures itself over every power plant, every pipeline, every substation will never be able to face the harder conflicts—foreign or domestic—and resolve them together.

We have to do better. We have to site these facilities fairly, negotiate these deals honestly, and stop treating communities as obstacles to be overcome. This book shows you how to make that happen where you live.

———

If you are holding this book, you are probably weeks or months into a process that will reshape your community for decades. You need answers, not just analysis.

Maybe a rezoning notice showed up in the mail. Maybe your electric bill jumped and nobody could explain why. Maybe the governor announced a "historic partnership" and nobody asked you first. Maybe you are the township supervisor making this decision with a staff of three and no outside counsel.

However you found out, the feeling is the same. You are angry. You are confused. You feel like the decision already got made without you.

I am not going to tell you to calm down. But I need to be honest with you about some things before we start.

———

I do not think all data centers are bad. I say that as someone with a foot on both sides of this fight.

My wife and I live on a small Michigan farmstead where a proposed 345 kV transmission line would cut through land a few hundred yards from our century-old bank barn. I know what it feels like when the infrastructure shows up in your backyard uninvited. But I also spent years working in the industries behind this buildout—AI research, finance, national security. I run the ALEA Institute, a small nonprofit focused on responsible AI, and I was part of the team that tested GPT-4 against the bar exam in 2022 and 2023. I know how these deals get made, and I know where the pressure points are.

AI could help cure cancer. It could accelerate fusion energy research and improve weather forecasting. These are not fantasies.

Real labs are doing real work on hard problems, and that work requires enormous computing power. The compute has to go somewhere. I have no interest in pretending otherwise. I used AI tools to help research and edit this very book.

I am also an American who believes a strong, stable America is good for the world. The national security case for AI is real. Geopolitics does not pause while communities sort out how they feel about substations and cooling towers. The defense and intelligence communities are planning for advanced AI systems that arrive within years, not decades. American AI capability matters.

But the rush to build massive new facilities is not the only path forward. If we are going to put a hand on the scale through government incentives, we should at least aim them in the right direction.

Fund models efficient enough to run on existing hardware in the thousands of data centers already connected to power and roads. Invest in architectures more efficient than today's generation of AI software. Reward companies that build smaller, specialized models for specific tasks instead of scaling everything to the sky. Steer facilities toward old industrial sites and contaminated land—places where drawing polluted groundwater for cooling might actually help the cleanup instead of draining a clean aquifer.

The national interest argues for AI capability. It does not argue for a race to pour concrete wherever the transmission lines happen to run.

———

There is one more thing you should know before we start, because it shapes the advice in every chapter that follows: I am genuinely worried about where this is going.

Some of the people building these systems are not sure where the technology will land, and some of their own researchers worry openly about the consequences. If the people designing AI are uncertain about the outcomes, your community should not be absorbing the downside risk based on their optimistic projections.

The labor market effects are already visible—not just where the data centers get built, but everywhere. Entire categories of work are being automated faster than anyone expected two years ago: customer service, claims processing, content writing, entry-level programming. That disruption is not caused by the building in your backyard. It is caused by the technology inside it, and it reaches every community whether or not a data center sits nearby.

But your community is being asked to bear the physical costs of that infrastructure—the noise, the water draw, the strain on the grid. That gives you standing to demand that the deal include something real. Local hiring commitments, direct community payments, and transition funds for workers whose industries shrink belong in every negotiation. If a company profits from automation while asking your town to absorb the cost of its operations, the least it can do is share the upside.

AI companies talk about curing cancer and solving climate change in their pitch decks and earnings calls. But much of their actual investment goes into chatbots designed to maximize your screen time and advertising systems designed to track your behavior. The gap between what the industry promises and what it delivers should make any community skeptical of the promises being made to get a local project approved.

The financial picture is fragile. Many developers have committed to projects they can barely finance. Interest rates rose faster than their models assumed. Demand projections for AI compute have softened in some segments. Power costs and water costs keep climbing.

Some developers have privately acknowledged that community rejection gives them a face-saving exit from deals that no longer pencil out. The irony should not escape you: in some cases, you may be fighting harder to stop the project than its own backers are fighting to build it.

None of this means data centers are going away. It means the terms on which they get built matter enormously. And right now, those terms are being set without you.

That is why this book exists.

"Fight" in the title does not mean only "stop." It means the full spectrum of engagement. Stop the project if it should not be built here. Negotiate better terms if it will be built regardless.

Demand ongoing monitoring after construction. Enforce the promises that were made to get it approved. Hold everyone to what they said on the record: the developer, the utility, your own elected officials.

Many local officials are trying to do the right thing with limited information and limited staff. Officials need it too. The goal is to give both residents and officials the tools to hold the developer to its promises. The deal should work for the community, not just the balance sheet.

The developer has a team of lawyers, consultants, and lobbyists who have done this dozens of times. Your township has a part-time planner and a solicitor who also handles zoning variances for backyard sheds. That imbalance is not an accident. It is the business model. What follows helps close the gap.

Some communities have negotiated deals that delivered meaningful tax revenue, local jobs, and enforceable environmental protections. The chapters ahead show you how to be one of them. A community that sits out the process gets whatever terms were set without its input.

Here is how the book is organized.

Chapters 1 and 2 orient you. They explain what data centers are, how the industry works, who the major players are, and why this particular project landed in your community. Chapters 3 through 5 cover government levers at every level: local, state, and federal. Each chapter walks through what elected officials, regulatory agencies, and courts can do—and what they cannot.

Chapters 6 and 7 cover private legal and contractual tools: property rights, nuisance claims, community benefit agreements, and tax clawbacks. Chapter 8 covers market pressure: how to use a company's own public commitments and financial promises against it when those promises get broken. Chapter 9 is about organizing: building coalitions, working with the press, and running community education campaigns. Chapter 10 ties everything together into a multi-front strategy for the long game.

Three appendices provide reference materials: a glossary of terms, sample documents you can adapt, and a directory of organizations that can help.

You do not need to read every chapter. Start with Chapters 1 and 2, then jump to whichever chapter matches your strongest lever. A routing guide at the end of Chapter 1 will point you there.

A companion book, *This Is Server Country*, tells the full story of the buildout—the money, the machines, the politics, the people caught in the middle. That book explains *why* this is happening. This one tells you *what to do* about it.

Your next planning board meeting is probably a few weeks away. Let's get you ready.

You Just Found Out

On February 10, 2026, a standing-room-only crowd packed a government meeting hall in Fulton County, Indiana. Many wore "NO Data Center" hats and T-shirts. Each attendee got two minutes to speak. The meeting stretched for hours.

Most of them had learned about the project from a TV interview. Indiana's governor had said, almost in passing, that Fulton County "would love to have a data center." No one in the room remembered saying that.

A Chicago-based developer called Decennial Group wanted to build a 500-megawatt facility on 300 acres of farmland.

Terms in gray boxes are defined the first time they appear.

Megawatt	A unit of electrical power. One megawatt can power about 800 homes. A 500-megawatt data center uses as much electricity as a small city.

The Area Plan Commission had already changed the zoning ordinance to allow data centers on agricultural land. One resident put it simply: "It was passed and I still don't know how that happened without anyone knowing."

If something like this just happened in your community, this book is for you.

No matter how you found out, you are facing the same problem: a project with billion-dollar backing and a public process that moves faster than you can follow. The decision seems like it already happened. The details are hard to find. The people who should be answering your questions are not returning calls.

You have a vote, a public records law, and a right to speak at every hearing. That is more than the developer expects you to use. But you need to move fast, and you need to know where to push.

1.1 What a Data Center Actually Is

A data center is a building full of computer servers. That one sentence is the last simple thing about them.

A modern "hyperscale" data center is an industrial building the size of several football fields. Inside: thousands of servers, networking gear, backup generators, and cooling systems. From the outside, it looks like a giant windowless warehouse behind a security fence.

These buildings run 24 hours a day, 365 days a year. They never close for holidays. They never go quiet at night. They power the cloud services, AI systems, and online tools that make billions for the world's largest tech companies. The artificial intelligence boom that started in 2023 has made data centers the fastest-growing category of industrial construction in the country.

The scale is hard to overstate. As of early 2026, the U.S. data center construction pipeline exceeds $88 billion in projects set to start within six months. Chapter 2 explains who is spending the money and why.

1.1.1 What It Looks Like

The industry's own term is "blank box"—blank walls, no windows, concrete block or metal panels. The proposed Digital Gateway project in Prince William County, Virginia, spans 2,100 acres and up to 37 buildings. That is about 150 Walmart Supercenters.

At night, security lighting makes the site glow like a stadium visible from miles away. Drive by any data center campus and count the cars in the parking lot. It will not take long. These buildings employ very few people.

1.1.2 What It Sounds Like

Data centers are loud.

The cooling fans, air handlers, and chillers produce a constant hum at 55 to 85 decibels—like a vacuum cleaner that never turns off. That sound runs day and night, every day of the year.

When backup generators kick on during power outages or routine testing, noise levels can reach 100 to 110 decibels at the source—about as loud as a chainsaw.

In Aurora, Illinois, residents near a CyrusOne data center describe the experience in physical terms. "You can hear it as soon as you walk out," one resident said. "Fans, just constant with the noise. You feel it in your bones." Sound walls installed by the company "do not help much" because the noise comes from rooftop equipment.

Low-frequency hum penetrates walls and windows. Closing your windows does not fix it. Your brain cannot tune it out the way it tunes out traffic or wind. Chapter 2 covers the health research on long-term noise exposure.

1.1.3 What It Uses

The impact of a data center boils down to five things: electricity, water, land, jobs, and air quality.

Electricity. A single facility uses as much power as a small city—and rising demand is raising everyone's bills.

Water. Facilities that use evaporative cooling consume millions of gallons per day from the same supply as farms and homes. That water evaporates—it does not come back. Even facilities that do not draw water for cooling can lower water tables or disrupt drainage when hundreds of acres of farmland are cleared, graded, and paved.

Land. Hundreds of acres of farmland, permanently converted. Once cleared and paved, it is not going back to farming in your lifetime. And the building is only part of the footprint. A data center campus also needs transmission lines, substations, and often solar farms or battery storage to supply its power. Those projects consume additional land—sometimes in communities miles from the data center itself.

Jobs. A single data center can cover dozens of acres but employ fewer people than a mid-size restaurant.

Air. Backup diesel generators produce pollutants linked to asthma and cancer. In Southaven, Mississippi, xAI installed 27 gas turbines without obtaining air permits in a community that already faced pollution levels far above the national average.

Chapter 2 breaks down the numbers behind each of these.

Developer, tenant, utility	Three players appear throughout this book. The **developer** builds the facility and negotiates zoning and tax deals with your local government. The **tenant**—usually a tech giant like Amazon, Google, or Microsoft—runs the servers inside and often dictates the timeline. The **utility** upgrades the grid to deliver power and passes those costs to all ratepayers. Knowing which one you are dealing with changes your strategy.

1.2   How Communities Find Out

You probably did not get a formal notice. You heard a rumor, saw a news story, or noticed heavy equipment on a road that used to be quiet. That is the norm, not the exception.

A note on local government: depending on your state, the local government with authority over zoning and land use may be a city, a township, a village, a county, or a borough. This book uses "local government" to mean whichever body controls zoning where the project is proposed.

Data center developers typically keep projects quiet during site selection. By the time the project is public, land purchases, zoning changes, and tax deals are often already complete. Here are the five most common ways people learn a data center is coming:

1. A rezoning application appears. A rezoning application is the most common trigger. The developer files to change how a piece of land is zoned—say, from farm use to light industrial. That filing creates a public record. It may also trigger a notice to neighboring property owners. In Coweta County, Georgia, residents learned about Project Sail—a $17 billion, 831-acre campus—through a state development filing.

Search your city, township, or county planning office website for pending applications.

2. A public official mentions it. A governor, a township supervisor, a county commissioner, or an economic development director mentions the project in a press event—before residents have been told. That is what happened in Fulton County, Indiana.

Request the meeting recording or minutes from your municipal or county clerk.

3. Reporters or residents notice land transactions. Large purchases of contiguous parcels by a shell company often signal a data center.

Shell company	A business that exists only on paper, used to hide who really owns a project. Developers set up LLCs with names like "Maple Leaf Holdings" so their real name does not appear in county records.

Developers use LLCs and holding companies to hide the real buyer. Google's Chesterfield County, Virginia, project was filed under the name "Project Peanut." Amazon's Pima County, Arizona, project was filed as "Project Blue." If you see a name like "Project Galaxy" or "Maple Leaf Holdings LLC" in property records, search the name online. Sometimes a filing in another jurisdiction or a corporate registration will reveal the real company behind it.

Search your county recorder's or assessor's website for recent large land sales to unfamiliar LLCs.

4. An NDA expires or leaks. Many developers require local officials to sign nondisclosure agreements before sharing project details. The deals are meant to prevent "bidding wars" between towns—but they also keep residents in the dark about what their own government is doing.

File a public records request for any NDAs your local government has signed. See below for how.

5. The facility already exists and gets worse. Some residents learn about the problem not from a new proposal but from an existing facility getting bigger or louder. In Aurora, Illinois, a CyrusOne campus expanded until the noise from its cooling systems could be felt inside neighboring homes.

Check your local government's approved permits for expansion plans already in the pipeline.

Marana, Arizona, shows how the pattern plays out. Tucson-area residents learned about a proposed 600-acre data center weeks before a town vote on rezoning the land. The developer, operating through a subsidiary called Fremont Peak Properties, never publicly identified the end user. At the December 2025 planning commission meeting, more than 20 community members spoke against the project. The commission approved it 6–0. Residents collected 2,800 petition signatures for a voter referendum. The town rejected the petitions on a technicality: they did not include the legal description of the properties, which Arizona requires for zoning referenda. The lesson: know your state's petition requirements *before* you start collecting signatures.

1.2.1 *The NDA Problem*

Nondisclosure agreements between local governments and data center developers are common. They change what your officials can legally tell you—and when.

A study of Virginia municipalities found that 25 of 31 localities with existing or proposed data centers had signed NDAs with developers. In Michigan, at least four communities signed NDAs related to data center proposals. One community, Menomonie, Wisconsin, signed an NDA in February 2024—more than a year before publicly announcing a $1.6 billion project. During that year, the city quietly approved predevelopment agreements and created a special tax district without mentioning the data center in meeting agendas or minutes.

NDAs bar officials from sharing "business plans" and "non-public information." They often instruct officials to share "as little as legally possible." They require advance notice to the company so its legal team can intervene before any disclosure.

The result: your elected officials may know a data center is coming and be barred by contract from telling you.

If you suspect an NDA is in place, file a public records request. The existence of an NDA between a public entity and a private company is itself a public record in most states. You will not get the project details the NDA protects, but you can confirm the agreement exists and learn who signed it and when.

Officials can push back. In St. Charles, Missouri, the mayor declared "there will never be another NDA" after a data center proposal collapsed amid public distrust. Pima County, Arizona, adopted a 90-day sunshine rule: project details must be disclosed at least 90 days before any public vote.

Ohio and Michigan legislators have introduced bills to ban local officials from signing NDAs at all. If an official tells you they cannot share project information because of an NDA, that answer deserves scrutiny. See Chapter 3 for what to demand and how to file records requests.

> **⚠ Caution**
>
> NDAs do not override open meetings laws. If your governing body voted on anything related to the project in a closed session, that vote may have been illegal. See Chapter 3 for how to challenge open meetings violations.

1.2.2 How to Spot the Next One

If you have already been through one data center fight, you can catch the next project earlier.

Watch the planning agenda. Check your county or city planning office website weekly. Rezoning applications and conditional use permit filings appear on the agenda before any notice is mailed.

Search utility filings. Large data centers must apply to connect to the grid. Search your state utility commission's website for interconnection applications. In PJM states, check the PJM interconnection queue at https://www.pjm.com. A 100-megawatt application near your town is an early signal.

Set alerts. A Google News alert for "data center" plus your county name costs nothing and catches press releases, land transactions, and news stories as they appear.

Check land records. Rapid purchases of contiguous farmland parcels by an LLC you have never heard of may signal a project. Search your county recorder's website for recent large land sales.

1.3 WHAT HAPPENS NEXT

If a project has been announced, the timeline usually follows a predictable sequence. Your position in the process determines how much time you have and which tools are still available.

Phase 1: Site selection (6–18 months before public announcement). The developer identifies candidate sites based on power availability, land cost, tax incentives, and permitting speed. Site selection happens behind closed doors. Officials may sign NDAs. You will not know about it unless someone leaks or a land transaction shows up in public records. Set up the surveillance steps in "How to Spot the Next One" above to catch projects at this stage.

Phase 2: Announcement and approvals (1–6 months). The project becomes public, usually through a rezoning application, a press release, or a public official's comment. The announcement phase is when hearings get scheduled and public comment periods open. For most communities, this is the first chance to engage. It is also the period with the most bargaining power.

Developers are on a tight schedule. Every month of delay costs them money and risks losing their position in the utility's interconnection queue. That urgency is your advantage.

They need approvals. You have questions. See Chapter 3 for how to demand conditions before any vote.

Phase 3: Permitting and preconstruction (3–12 months). After zoning approval, the developer applies for building permits, environmental permits, utility interconnection, and water permits. Each permit is a separate opportunity for public comment or legal challenge. See Chapter 6 and Chapter 7 for how to use them.

Phase 4: Construction (18–36 months). Site clearing, grading, and building. Once construction starts, stopping the project becomes much harder. Legal challenges can still succeed, but the developer will argue reliance on existing approvals. Focus on permit violations and environmental enforcement—see Chapter 5.

Phase 5: Operation and expansion. The facility goes live. Data centers are built in phases—a campus approved for 100 megawatts today may grow to 500 megawatts over a decade. If the first phase was approved with weak conditions, every expansion follows the same weak terms. The conditions you negotiate at Phase 2 set the rules for everything that comes after.

>  **Tip**
>
> If you are in Phase 1 or 2, your most powerful tool is a moratorium. A moratorium is a temporary pause on new permits that gives your community time to study the project and set rules. See Chapter 3 for how to request one. If you are in Phase 3 or later, focus on permit conditions and legal challenges. See Chapter 6 and Chapter 7.

1.4 YOU ARE NOT ALONE

If you feel blindsided, you are in large company.

As of early 2026, at least 99 local governments in 24 states have enacted data center moratoria, and dozens more have considered them. The backlash is not a fringe movement. It is happening in rural counties in Indiana, suburban townships across Michigan, mid-size cities like Aurora, Illinois, and major cities like New Orleans.

Between May 2024 and June 2025, organized community opposition blocked or delayed more than $160 billion worth of data center projects. Lawmakers took notice: in 2025, legislators in all 50 states considered at least 238 data center-related bills, enacting over 40 new laws on noise, water reporting, and tax break reform.

Communities that organized changed outcomes. In Prince George's County, Maryland, a petition with over 22,500 signatures pushed the county executive to issue a 180-day moratorium. In Warrenton, Virginia, the four council members who approved data center zoning either lost their seats or chose not to run. The new council banned data centers 6–0 (see Chapter 10). The opposition cuts across party lines (see Chapter 9).

Other communities have already tested every tool in this book. National organizations like Data Center Watch, Kairos Fellowship, and Food & Water Watch connect communities with experienced organizers and legal resources (see Appendix C). This book collects their strategies so you can use them.

1.5 How This Book Works

Start with Chapter 2 to understand the project and evaluate the developer's claims. Then go to the chapter that matches your situation:

- **The project still needs a zoning vote or permit?** Start with Chapter 3—local zoning, moratoria, public comment, elections.
- **Your electric bill is the concern?** Start with Chapter 4—utility rate cases, state legislation.
- **Noise, light, or water affecting your property?** Start with Chapter 6—nuisance claims, water rights, finding a lawyer.
- **A tax break or incentive deal is on the table?** Start with Chapter 7—community benefit agreements, clawbacks, conditions.
- **Federal permits or environmental review involved?** Start with Chapter 5—Clean Water Act, EPA, FERC.
- **Want to pressure the company directly?** Start with Chapter 8—shareholder activism, ESG campaigns.
- **Building a coalition?** Start with Chapter 9—organizing, press strategy, elections.
- **Fighting on multiple fronts?** Chapter 10 shows how to combine strategies.

Every chapter works on its own, with cross-references to related material. The appendices include a glossary (Appendix A), sample documents you can adapt (Appendix B), and a resource list (Appendix C).

1.5.1 A Note on Uncertainty

This book is not anti-technology or anti-development. It is anti-getting-a-bad-deal-without-knowing-it.

Some communities have concluded that the costs outweigh the benefits and fought to stop projects entirely. Others negotiated better terms and considered the result a win. Both are legitimate outcomes.

What this book does is help you ask the right questions. The central question, at every stage, is this: *If the optimistic projection is wrong, who bears the downside risk?*

16

Chapter 2 applies this question to every major claim developers make—jobs, electricity, water, tax revenue, and technology risk—and shows you what to ask.

You should not have to bear the risk of someone else's uncertainty. That is not an anti-development position. It is a pro-accountability position.

The companies building these facilities have thousands of lawyers and lobbyists, and they have done this hundreds of times. You are doing it for the first time. The chapters that follow give you tools to hold them accountable.

> ### ☑ What You Can Do
>
> **First steps—do these within your first week of learning about the project:**
>
> 1. **Get the project number.** Call the planning office for your city, township, village, or county—whichever has zoning authority over the site. Ask for the application number, the developer's name, and the hearing date. Write them down.
>
> 2. **Request the application.** Ask the same office for the conditional use permit or rezoning application, the site plan, and any environmental or traffic studies. These are public documents. Most offices will email a PDF.
>
> 3. **Find the comment deadline.** Check your local government's website under "Planning & Zoning" or "Public Notices." Written comments become part of the legal record even if you also speak at the hearing.
>
> 4. **Find your neighbors.** Talk to the people on your street. See if anyone else knows what is happening. You need at least two or three people willing to attend the next public meeting.
>
> 5. **Read Chapter 2.** Before the first hearing, understand what the developer is promising and how to evaluate those claims.

What You're Up Against

In December 2024, Virginia's legislature learned what its own tax breaks were worth. The state had given data centers more than $1.6 billion in sales tax exemptions that year alone—and its auditors studied what taxpayers got in return. For every dollar Virginia gave up, it got back forty-eight cents. The state concluded the program "does not pay for itself."

Virginia is the data center capital of the world. Loudoun County hosts more data centers than any place on earth. If any state should have gotten a good deal, it was Virginia. It didn't.

Before you attend your first hearing, before you read the developer's glossy brochure, you need to understand what you are dealing with. Not the building. The business.

2.1 WHO BUILDS DATA CENTERS

Three kinds of companies are involved in every data center project. You will probably deal with one or two of them. All three make decisions that affect your community.

2.1.1 The Tenants: Big Tech

The companies whose software actually runs inside data centers are called hyperscalers. They are the reason the building exists.

Amazon, Microsoft, and Google control about 63% of global cloud revenue. Together with Meta and Oracle, those five companies spent more than $440 billion on data center and AI infrastructure in 2025.

A newer group of AI companies—CoreWeave, xAI, OpenAI—is building at enormous scale, often in communities that have never seen a data center.

For context: the entire U.S. spent about $143 billion on highway and bridge construction in 2024. The data center buildout is more than three times that—in a single year. By some measures, this is the largest concentrated infrastructure buildout in American history since the interstate highway system. Unlike the interstates, it is almost entirely privately funded.

2.1.2 The Builders: Operators and Developers

The company that shows up to your planning board meeting is usually not Google or Amazon. It is an operator—a company that builds, owns, and runs the physical building. Operators lease space and power to the hyperscalers.

Names you might see on a permit application: Digital Realty, Equinix, QTS, Compass, Vantage, CyrusOne, Switch, Aligned, Stream, or CloudHQ. Some are publicly traded. Others are owned by private equity firms. CoreWeave blurs the line—it is both a tenant running AI workloads and an operator building its own facilities.

When a representative from Compass Data Centers walks into a county planning meeting, you should know: Compass builds for Microsoft, Google, and Meta. The actual tenant's name may never appear on any local filing.

2.1.3 The Money: Private Equity

Behind many operators sits a private equity firm or infrastructure fund.

Private equity	Investment firms that pool money from wealthy investors and pension funds to buy and run companies. They are not traded on the stock market and disclose far less than public companies.

These firms provide the capital and set the deal terms. They are usually invisible to the community.

Blackstone owns QTS and holds over $70 billion in data center assets. These firms manage pension fund money, sovereign wealth fund money, and insurance company reserves. They expect 15–25% annual returns. That return expectation drives every decision about your community.

Your community is a line item in a portfolio—a site selected because it offered available power, cheap land, and willing officials. The company at your planning board meeting is a subsidiary of a subsidiary. The person who decided to build in your county may work in an office in Manhattan.

Look up the company on the permit application. Search for "[company name] parent company" or "[company name] investor." If the applicant is an LLC, search your state's business registry for the registered agent. That trail usually leads to one of the firms described above.

2.2 WHY YOUR COMMUNITY

Your community was not chosen because the developer admires your schools or your workforce. It was chosen for one reason above all others: power.

2.2.1 Power Comes First

The industry calls it "power-first development." Site selection starts with available electricity—not customers, not workforce, not quality of life. In a 2025 survey, 84% of data center decision-makers ranked power availability among their top three factors.

The reason is simple. A data center needs a direct connection to the high-voltage grid. Building new transmission lines takes five to ten years. A site that already has 100 megawatts of available substation capacity is worth more than a site with cheaper land and no power.

If your community has a nearby power plant, a large substation, or a retiring coal or gas facility, that is why the developer is here. Not because of your schools. Not because of your workforce. Because of the wires.

The waiting list to connect to the power grid, called the "interconnection queue," averages five to ten years. A site that already has available power skips that line. That is worth billions to a developer operating on a two-year build schedule.

2.2.2 What Else Matters

After power, the list looks like this:

1. **Fiber connectivity.** Proximity to major fiber routes. Less important for AI training facilities, more important for cloud services.

2. **Land.** Hyperscale campuses need 100 to 500 or more acres of flat, buildable land. Farmland fits the bill. Data centers are not the only infrastructure converting agricultural land—solar farms, wind turbines, transmission lines, and battery storage all face the same tension. The difference: a data center triggers demand for many of these at once, requiring new transmission corridors, generation, and substations across multiple counties. The question is the same for any of them: who decides where it goes, and who bears the cost?

3. **Tax incentives.** At least 36 states now offer targeted data center tax breaks, up from roughly 20 a decade ago.

4. **Water.** Traditional cooling systems consume millions of gallons per year. Regions with abundant water are preferred.

5. **Permitting speed.** States like Indiana and West Virginia created fast-track permitting. Developers prize speed.

6. **Political climate.** Communities that have passed moratoria get avoided— or get offered larger benefit packages.

Many of these target communities—small townships, unincorporated counties, rural towns that have never seen a billion-dollar proposal—lack zoning codes and negotiating experience for projects this large. That is not an accident. It is site selection strategy. Ask your planning office whether the developer cited available power capacity as a reason for choosing your community. If they did, ask who paid for that infrastructure.

2.3 WHAT GETS PROMISED

Every data center proposal comes with a pitch. The pitch has three parts: jobs, tax revenue, and economic growth. Each one deserves a closer look.

2.3.1 Jobs

The jobs number is the most misleading claim in most data center proposals.

Construction jobs are real but temporary. A large data center hires 1,000 to 2,500 workers during construction, which lasts 18 to 24 months. Once the building is done, those workers leave.

Permanent jobs are the number that matters. A typical 250,000-square-foot data center employs about 50 full-time workers, and half of those are contractors. A facility that covers 100 acres might have fewer people on site than a mid-size restaurant.

> **ⓘ Key Fact**
>
> Across states that track this data, data centers create roughly 30 to 50 permanent jobs per $1 billion invested. A corporate headquarters or manufacturing plant with the same fiscal impact would create far more permanent jobs and far more local spending.

For every permanent job, data centers typically create several times as many temporary construction positions. When the developer says "500 jobs," ask: how many are permanent?

Food & Water Watch found that as few as 23,000 people may have worked in U.S. data centers as of 2024—far fewer than the industry's claim of 600,000. The gap comes from counting construction, supply chain, and indirect employment. The direct count, people who show up every day, is much smaller.

2.3.2 Tax Revenue

The developer's economic impact study will project millions in annual tax revenue. That projection rarely mentions the tax breaks.

States compete for data centers by offering sales tax exemptions on equipment, property tax abatements, and other incentives.

Tax abatement	A deal where the government reduces or eliminates a company's taxes for a set number of years. Abatements can apply to property taxes, sales taxes on equipment, or both. The idea is to attract the company, but the lost revenue has to be made up somewhere—usually by other taxpayers.

At least 36 states offer some version of these breaks. The total cost is staggering.

Virginia's sales tax exemption for data centers cost $685 million in 2023, $1 billion in 2024, and $1.6 billion in 2025. Texas revised its cost estimate from

$130 million to over $1 billion in just 23 months. Illinois saw its exemption costs grow from $10 million in 2020 to $370 million in 2023—a 3,600% increase in three years.

Every state that has studied its return on investment has found a loss. Virginia gets back 48 cents for every dollar it gives up. Washington and Georgia lose 60 to 70 cents on the dollar. Georgia's own auditors found that 70% of data center construction would have happened without any tax break at all.

Ohio's numbers tell the story. The state approved 13 data center tax agreements between 2017 and 2024. Companies committed to invest $5.1 billion and create 356 permanent jobs—more than $965,000 in public subsidies per permanent job. Ohio also offers property tax abatements of 65–100% for 15 to 30 years. A company that builds a $2 billion facility may pay almost no property tax for a generation. The schools, the fire department, and the roads still need funding. But the tax revenue that would have paid for them never arrives.

Indiana offers the longest incentives in the country: up to 50 years of sales tax exemptions for investments over $750 million. Michigan's incentives can run through 2050 or 2065. These commitments outlast the technology, the company's business plan, and in some cases the building itself.

In February 2026, Illinois Governor Pritzker proposed freezing the state's data center tax incentive program for two years after costs grew from $10 million to $370 million in three years. Other states are watching.

2.3.3 *What They Don't Tell You*

Fewer than half the states with incentive programs disclose how much revenue they give up. Only 11 disclose which companies receive the benefits. Not a single state tracks both jobs promised and jobs delivered.

 **Tip**

When the developer presents an economic impact study at a public hearing, ask three questions:

1. Who commissioned and paid for this study?
2. Does the analysis include the cost of the tax breaks as a subtraction from net revenue?
3. Has the methodology been reviewed by anyone not employed by the developer?

If the answer to any of these is no, say so on the record. It matters when the deal comes up for review.

Virginia, Texas, Georgia, and Illinois alone give up more than $3 billion per year in data center tax breaks, and many states do not disclose their costs at all.

Foregone revenue	Tax money the government chose not to collect because of a tax break. It is money that would have gone to schools, roads, and services.

Every dollar in foregone revenue is a dollar your community has to raise from other sources—or go without.

2.4 WHO PAYS

The costs of a data center do not appear on the developer's fact sheet. They show up on your electric bill, your water bill, and your property tax statement.

2.4.1 *Your Electric Bill*

Data centers consumed 4.4% of all U.S. electricity in 2023, a share projected to reach 6.7 to 12% by 2028. Someone has to pay for the grid to keep up. In the short and medium term, that means higher bills. Some analysts argue that increased demand will attract new generation and eventually lower prices—but "eventually" does not help you when the rate increase hits next year.

> **Ratepayer** — Anyone who pays an electric or water bill. When a utility spends money on grid upgrades, ratepayers are the ones who cover the cost through higher bills.

In PJM, the grid operator serving 13 states from New Jersey to Illinois, data center demand was the largest single factor in the price increase in the 2025/2026 capacity auction. Monthly bills rose $16 to $21 in some PJM zones.

A Carnegie Mellon study cited in a Senate investigation found that electricity prices in central and Northern Virginia could rise 25% by 2030 because of data center demand. Amazon funded a study arguing data centers do not raise bills. When you see a study about data center impacts, check who paid for it. And when someone promises that long-term benefits will offset short-term costs, ask: who absorbs the loss if the long-term benefits never arrive?

More than 30 states now have "large-load tariffs" designed to prevent data centers from shifting costs to residential customers. See Chapter 4 for how these tariffs work and how to push for them.

2.4.2 *Your Water*

Most large data centers use evaporative cooling, which works like sweat: water absorbs heat and evaporates. That water is gone. Some newer facilities use air-cooled or liquid-cooled systems that draw little or no water—but even those projects can affect local water. Clearing and paving hundreds of acres changes how rain drains, and excavation near wetlands or floodplains can lower the water table in neighboring wells. The question is: who gets the water when there is not enough to go around?

The proposed Project Sail in Coweta County, Georgia, would use up to 9 million gallons daily—roughly one-third of the county's allocation from the Chattahoochee River. Google's Mesa, Arizona, facility has a permit to draw up to 4 million gallons per day in a region that gets 8 inches of rain per year.

Most data center water contracts guarantee a fixed daily allocation that does not change in a drought year. Your lawn watering restrictions change. Your farm's irrigation allotment changes. The data center's contract does not.

At least eight states have introduced water reporting bills. Governors in California and Virginia vetoed them; New Jersey's governor issued a conditional veto.

2.4.3   *Your Property*

No peer-reviewed study has measured how data centers affect nearby property values in rural or suburban markets. Developers cite this absence as evidence of no harm. Neighbors who live next to constant noise, backup generators, and security lighting know better.

One George Mason University study found higher home prices near data centers in Northern Virginia—but that is a mature market where data centers brought infrastructure to already-developed areas. That finding may not apply to a 300-acre facility on farmland next to your subdivision.

Get a professional appraisal before construction begins. Photograph your property and neighborhood. Save real estate listings for comparable homes. This documentation supports a future claim if values drop. See Chapter 6 for how to handle property value claims.

2.4.4   *Your Air*

Every data center has backup diesel generators that produce nitrogen oxides, particulate matter, and formaldehyde. A UC Riverside and Caltech study projected that all data center-related air pollution could contribute to an estimated 1,300 premature deaths per year by 2028. The projected cost: $12 to $21 billion per year in health impacts, under continued growth assumptions. Virginia alone has permitted about 8,000 diesel generators for data centers.

Ask any developer: how many backup generators will the facility have? What fuel do they use? How many hours per year will they run? Find the air permit application on your state environmental agency's website, or ask your county planning office. If no application has been filed, ask why.

Where data centers cluster, the cumulative effect is worst. Individual permits may comply with the law. The combined impact may not. If your community already has data centers, demand a cumulative air quality study before a new permit is approved.

2.5 How the Deal Gets Done

Chapter 1 described the five phases of a data center project. What matters here is what happens before you hear about it. By the time the project is announced, the developer has already chosen your community, secured state incentives, and often reached preliminary agreements with local officials.

2.5.1 The Information Gap

The developer has done this dozens of times. They have lawyers, lobbyists, and economic impact studies prepared by firms they hired. They secured the state incentives before the first public hearing.

Your planning board may be staffed by volunteers. You have days or weeks to respond to what took the developer months to prepare. The developer's environmental consultant, economic impact study, and lawyer all work for the developer.

The developer is not necessarily lying. They are presenting a carefully constructed case, funded by their own money, delivered on their own timeline. Your job is to slow the process down long enough to ask the right questions.

What you have: a vote, standing, numbers (residents outnumber the developer's team a hundred to one), and time—if you use it. A moratorium gives the community months to study the proposal while the developer's clock keeps ticking. If a developer says "we need an answer by next month," that deadline is theirs, not yours. See Chapter 3 for how to request a moratorium.

2.6 The Question That Matters

The developer's projections may be right. The facility may create the promised jobs. The tax revenue may cover the cost of services. The cooling system may use less water than projected.

But what if the projections are wrong?

That is the question to ask at every stage of this process. Not whether the developer is lying—maybe they believe their own numbers. The question is: *if the optimistic projection turns out to be wrong, who absorbs the loss?*

2.6.1 *How to Apply It*

Take any claim the developer makes and ask two questions. What happens if this projection is right? And what happens if it is wrong—who pays?

Jobs. The developer projects 100 permanent jobs. If the projection is right, 100 people have good jobs. If it is wrong—and the facility creates 30 jobs instead—the tax break is already locked in. The community gave up revenue for jobs that did not appear.

Electricity. The developer says the project will not raise your electric bill. If the projection is right, rates stay stable. If it is wrong, and the utility commission allocates grid upgrade costs to all customers, every household in the service territory pays more. Ask who bears the risk of cost overruns. If the developer says prices will not go up, ask them to put that in writing.

Water. The facility's water projections assume average weather and a specific cooling technology. If there is a drought year, or if the operator switches to cheaper evaporative cooling, those projections are wrong. Ask for worst-case water numbers, not averages. Ask what happens to your water supply in a drought year when the data center's contract does not change but the reservoir level does.

Tax revenue. The developer promises $50 million in annual tax payments. If the abatement reduces the effective rate by 80%, the real payment is $10 million. If the abatement lasts 25 years, the community has locked itself into that number for a generation. Ask what happens if the company leaves before the abatement expires. Ask what the property is worth as a vacant industrial building. QTS told Iowa supervisors their data center buildings have a 20-year lifespan. Twenty years from now, who owns the cleanup?

Technology. The entire business case rests on continued demand for cloud computing and AI. If the market shifts, the facility becomes a stranded asset. The developer walks away. The building stays.

Ask about decommissioning bonds—who pays to demolish the building and restore the site if the company leaves? Almost no community requires one for data centers, even though solar farms and wind turbines routinely do. See Chapter 7 for how to negotiate these protections.

2.6.2 Not Anti-Development

Asking these questions is not anti-development. It is pro-accountability.

What is not legitimate is asking a community to accept all the downside risk while the developer keeps all the upside. That is not a partnership. It is a subsidy.

The rest of this book gives you tools to change that dynamic—from moratoria to shareholder proposals, from rate cases to elections. The developer is counting on you not knowing these tools exist.

The transfer runs in one direction. Ratepayers and taxpayers absorb the costs. The developer keeps the profits. The developer gets cheap land, cheap power, cheap water, and tax breaks. The community gets noise, diesel exhaust, higher electric bills, and a building that will be obsolete in 20 years.

Some communities have negotiated deals that include real tax revenue, environmental monitoring, and enforceable job guarantees. The difference between a good deal and a bad one is the subject of Chapter 7.

The companies building these facilities are among the wealthiest in human history—combined profits exceeding $325 billion in 2024. They can afford to meet community standards for noise, water, air quality, and fair taxation. If they say otherwise, they are negotiating, not stating facts.

You should not have to bear the risk of someone else's uncertainty.

> ### ✅ What You Can Do
>
> **Before the first hearing, get answers to these five questions:**
>
> 1. **Ask how many permanent jobs the facility will create**—not construction jobs—and what the cost per job is in tax breaks (see Chapter 7 for clawback provisions).
>
> 2. **Ask who funded the economic impact study**, whether it subtracts the cost of tax breaks from projected revenue, and whether anyone independent has reviewed it.
>
> 3. **Ask for peak water and electricity numbers, not averages**—and ask who pays for grid upgrades and what happens to the water supply in a drought year.
>
> 4. **Ask what the tax abatement is worth and how long it lasts**, then calculate what the property tax bill would be without it.
>
> 5. **Ask who the actual owner is**—not the LLC on the permit application—and whether there is a decommissioning bond if the company leaves.

CHAPTER THREE

Fight at City Hall

Loudoun County, Virginia, hosts more data centers than any place on earth. For years, data centers were built "by right" in industrial zones—meaning the developer filed a site plan and started building. No public hearing. No conditions. No community input.

On March 18, 2025, the Board of Supervisors voted 7–2 to end that. Every data center now requires a public hearing before the Planning Commission and another before the Board. Residents get to speak at both.

Planning commission	A group of appointed local residents who review building and land-use proposals. They hold public hearings and recommend whether the elected board should approve or deny a project.

If the county that hosts the most data centers in the world decided it needed more oversight, your community can too.

Zoning rules differ by state, but the strategy is the same everywhere. When a specific legal question matters—a deadline, a standing rule, an appeal right—check your local code or talk to a land-use lawyer.

3.1 The Zoning Code Is Your First Weapon

Zoning is the set of rules that controls what gets built where. Your county or city has a zoning code that divides land into zones: residential, commercial, industrial, agricultural. Each zone has a list of allowed uses.

Data centers live or die on how that list reads. If the code puts data centers in the wrong category, the developer builds without asking permission. If it puts them in the right category, the community gets a vote.

Everything in this section is about one thing: making sure your community has a vote.

3.1.1 By-Right vs. Conditional Use

The most important distinction in zoning law is between by-right uses and conditional uses.

A by-right use is automatic. If the zoning code says "data centers are permitted in industrial zones," the developer applies for a building permit and starts construction. The community has no say. The planning board holds no hearing. The building goes up.

A conditional use permit (also called a special use permit) works differently. The developer must apply. The planning staff reviews the application. A public hearing is scheduled. Residents can testify.

The planning board then votes on whether to approve or deny. The governing body, your board of supervisors or city council, votes. They can say no. They can attach conditions.

> **ⓘ Key Fact**
>
> If data centers are permitted by right in your community's industrial zones, you have no seat at the table. The single most important change you can push for is moving data centers from by-right to conditional use. Loudoun County proved it can be done.

3.1.2 The Definition Problem

Many zoning codes do not mention data centers at all. The code was written before anyone imagined a 100-acre building full of servers. Without one, the builder's lawyer will argue that a data center is a "warehouse" or an "office" or a "light industrial use"—whatever label lets them build by right.

The fix is to adopt a definition. A good one describes what the building does, not what it is called. One approach: "A facility primarily used for the storage, management, and processing of digital data, including associated power and cooling systems, occupying more than 10,000 square feet."

A size threshold matters. A small server closet in an office building is not what your community is trying to regulate. Communities have used thresholds ranging from 5,000 square feet to 10,000 square feet, or from 2 megawatts of power demand.

Once the definition is in the code, assign data centers to a zoning category that requires a conditional use permit. A conditional use requirement gives the community a vote on every project.

PennFuture published a free model ordinance covering water, power, noise, and aesthetic concerns. Download it and bring it to your next planning commission meeting. Other model ordinances are listed in Appendix C.

The PennFuture model defines "sensitive receptors"—schools, daycares, residential uses, and long-term care facilities—and requires greater setbacks and stricter noise limits near them. That language is ready to adopt.

3.1.3 *What If Data Centers Are Already By-Right?*

If your zoning code already allows data centers by right in industrial zones, you can still change it. A zoning text change modifies the code from that point on. Existing buildings and permits already filed are usually grandfathered. But every future application would require a hearing.

Loudoun County grandfathered applications filed before February 12, 2025, but required special exception approval for everything after. Fairfax County adopted its special exception requirement in September 2024 with a similar grandfather clause for projects in the pipeline before mid-July 2024.

The process for a zoning text amendment varies by state. In most towns, a resident can petition the planning commission or city council to start the amendment. The commission holds a public hearing, makes its suggestion, and the governing body votes.

The process is not fast. It can take three to six months. That is why a moratorium and a zoning text amendment often work together: the moratorium stops new applications while the text amendment moves through the process.

3.1.4   *If Your Community Has No Zoning Code*

Some rural townships have no zoning code at all. If yours is one of them, the local tools in this chapter are limited. Start with Chapter 4 for state-level options, and Chapter 9 for organizing.

3.1.5   *Conditions You Can Attach*

When a data center requires a conditional use permit, the governing body can attach conditions. These conditions become legally binding on the developer. Here are the ones that towns have used:

Setbacks. Distance from the building to the nearest property line. Standard industrial setbacks are often 50 feet. Communities have required 300 to 500 feet from residential properties.

Noise limits. Many towns use 60 decibels during the day and 55 at night, measured at the property line. See the Generators section below for generator-specific conditions.

Water. The developer should use municipal water, not private wells. Closed-loop cooling systems that recirculate water instead of evaporating it should be standard. A water impact study before approval is the minimum.

Visual impact. Ban barbed wire and razor wire fencing. Require landscaping buffers around the perimeter. Atlanta proposed banning aluminum siding and synthetic stucco on walls facing the public right-of-way.

Noise studies and monitoring. Require a sound study before approval and ongoing noise monitoring after the facility opens. If the facility exceeds the permitted noise level, the conditions should specify a remedy—not just a warning.

Lighting. Data centers run 24 hours a day and are lit accordingly. Security lighting on poles and buildings can produce glare visible from a mile away. Require fully shielded, downward-facing light fixtures that meet Dark-Sky standards. Limit light levels at the property line to 0.5 foot-candles. Ban uplighting.

Traffic. Construction generates heavy truck traffic for 12 to 18 months. A traffic impact study should be required before approval. Truck hours should be restricted: no heavy vehicles before 7 a.m. or after 7 p.m. on weekdays, and none on weekends. The developer should post a bond covering road repair costs and repair roads damaged during construction within 90 days of completion.

Rural roads were not built for the concrete trucks, steel haulers, and oversized loads that a data center project brings. If the developer does not pay for road damage, your county's road budget does.

Decommissioning. Data center buildings may be obsolete in 20 years. Require a decommissioning plan and a financial guarantee, such as a bond or escrow account. The guarantee should cover the cost of demolishing the facility and restoring the site if the operator leaves. Without this, the community is left with a giant empty building on former farmland and no money to clean it up.

Energy efficiency. Aurora, Illinois, proposed requiring data centers to meet a Power Usage Effectiveness (PUE) ratio of 1.2 or lower. PUE measures how well a facility uses power—a PUE of 1.2 means 20% of the power goes to cooling and overhead rather than computing. The lower the number, the more efficient the facility. Requiring a PUE standard pushes developers toward better technology and reduces total electricity demand.

Renewable energy. Some towns require developers to source a percentage of their electricity from renewable sources. The condition should say the energy must come from new sources within the same grid region—not from credits bought from a wind farm in another state. Specify rooftop, co-located, or brownfield installations where possible. Be honest about the trade-off: solar farms and wind turbines need land too, and the country needs more clean energy. But requiring new solar farms on farmland trades one land-use conflict for another. A good renewable energy condition addresses *where* the generation gets built, not just *whether* it exists.

Submit your proposed conditions in writing to the planning board before the hearing. Written proposals become part of the official record.

Note: The conditions you attach to a conditional use permit are legally binding and run with the land. If the developer sells the property, the new owner must honor them. Whether a neighbor can enforce those conditions directly varies by state—in some states, only the issuing authority can. Ask a land-use attorney about enforcement in your jurisdiction.

Generators. Require backup generators to meet EPA Tier 4 emission standards—the cleanest available. Limit generator testing to daytime hours. White County, Indiana, limits testing to 10 a.m. to 4 p.m. Require the developer to report generator run hours to the county quarterly.

See Chapter 7 for how these conditions relate to community benefit agreements.

3.2   The Moratorium

A moratorium is a temporary pause on new permits. It buys the community time to study the impacts and update the zoning code. If a data center project is moving faster than your community can respond, a moratorium is the emergency brake.

3.2.1   How It Works

Someone on the township board—or a resident at an open meeting—asks for a moratorium. The board directs the attorney to draft one. The attorney writes an ordinance that specifies what is paused (new data center applications), for how long (6 to 12 months is typical), and why (to study zoning and impacts).

Ordinance	A law passed by a local government—a city council, county board, or township. It works just like a state or federal law, but only within that jurisdiction.

The board holds a public hearing and votes.

In some towns, this takes two weeks. In others, two months.

3.2.2   What to Include

A weak moratorium is more likely to fail in court and waste the time you bought. A well-drafted moratorium has five elements.

1. Legal authority. The ordinance must cite the state law that gives your community the power to pause development. Some states have express moratorium statutes. North Carolina, Oregon, Washington, and California all have specific laws allowing moratoria. Other states rely on general police power—the government's authority to regulate for public health, safety, and welfare—or home rule authority. Your municipal attorney should know which applies.

2. Findings. The findings section is the most important. The findings explain why the moratorium is needed. They should name specific concerns: the community lacks zoning rules for data centers, the power grid has not been studied, the water supply has not been assessed.

Name noise, traffic, and property value impacts too. Strong findings tend to survive legal challenges. Weak findings tend to invite them. Use the central question from Chapter 2: *if the developer's projections are wrong, who bears the downside risk?*

3. Duration. Common ranges: 90 days for a quick study, 6 months for a serious one, 12 months for a full zoning code update. The Supreme Court has upheld temporary moratoria as valid, but those lasting more than a year face closer scrutiny. The safest approach is an "earlier of" clause: the moratorium expires on a fixed date *or* when the new regulations are adopted, whichever comes first.

4. Exemptions. Exempt projects that already have approved permits. Exempt existing facilities. Exempt small-scale uses below your size threshold. Exemptions reduce the risk that a court will strike the moratorium down.

5. A study requirement. The moratorium should direct the planning office (or a hired expert) to study data center impacts and suggest zoning rules. A study requirement gives the pause a purpose. Without it, the moratorium looks like a stall tactic.

White County, Indiana, shows what a moratorium can produce. The county passed a data center moratorium in October 2025. When it expired, White County adopted detailed regulations. The rules require EPA Tier 4 emission standards for backup generators, generator testing limited to 10 a.m. to 4 p.m., and a water impact study before approval. The county also added a 20-year property value guarantee: if a neighbor's property value drops because of the data center, the developer must make up the difference. That is the model: use the moratorium to study the problem and write rules that protect residents.

3.2.3 *Where Moratoria Are Happening*

As of early 2026, data center moratoria have been enacted in at least 24 states. Michigan alone has at least 26. You are not the first community to do this.

Act before a developer files an application. Once an application is in, the developer may argue "vested rights"—the claim that they should be judged under the rules that existed when they applied. If you see data center activity in a neighboring county, do not wait.

Any member of the governing body can propose a moratorium. If you cannot convince the full board, find one member who agrees. Even if the vote fails, it goes on the record.

In Prince George's County, Maryland, 22,500 residents signed a petition. The county passed a 180-day moratorium and used the time to draft permanent rules. That is the pattern: a moratorium buys time, and the community uses it to write stronger regulations.

3.2.4 *When Developers Sue*

Developers sometimes challenge moratoria or zoning denials in court. In most reported cases, they lose—but the lawsuit itself can be a weapon.

In Saline Township, Michigan, the board voted 4–1 to deny rezoning 575 acres of farmland for a $7 billion data center. The developer sued, alleging exclusionary zoning. The township settled within weeks, and the project—now under construction for Oracle and OpenAI—went through. A resident later challenged the settlement as a violation of the Open Meetings Act; a judge denied the challenge in February 2026, ruling it was filed too late.

Budget for legal costs if you pass a moratorium or deny a permit. A well-drafted ordinance with strong findings and a clear public purpose can hold up in court. That is why the findings section matters—it is your legal armor. Your municipal attorney should know this. If they are unsure, point them to *Moratorium Nation*, a free survey of data center moratoria that includes model ordinance language, at https://ssrn.com/abstract=6242898.

3.3 Updating Your Long-Range Plan

A moratorium buys time. The goal during that time is to update your zoning code and long-range plan.

A long-range plan (sometimes called a master plan) guides land use in your community. Courts give it weight when reviewing zoning decisions. If your plan says nothing about data centers, the developer can argue that your rules are random.

During the moratorium, ask your planning staff or a consultant to:

1. Identify which zones could hold data centers.
2. Study impacts on water, electricity, noise, and traffic.
3. Draft zoning standards—setbacks, noise limits, water restrictions, visual requirements.
4. Hold public meetings for resident input.

Albemarle County, Virginia, drafted standards with 60/55 dBA noise limits (day/night), closed-loop cooling rules, and facade design standards. Aurora, Illinois, proposed banning evaporative cooling, setting 59/49 dBA noise limits, and requiring chiller equipment to be at least 1,500 feet from residential property. Use the strongest provisions from other towns as your starting point.

3.4 PUBLIC RECORDS REQUESTS

If you suspect that your local government has been talking to a data center developer behind closed doors, you can find out. Public records requests— sometimes called FOIA requests—are your tool.

3.4.1 *What to Request*

Start with these:

1. **Nondisclosure agreements.** Any NDA between the locality and any developer, shell company, or technology company. NDAs between public entities and private companies are public records in most states.
2. **Emails.** All emails and letters between elected officials, planning staff, and any developer or consultant about data center development. In Festus, Missouri, emails obtained through records requests revealed months of secret contact between officials and the developer—and triggered a recall effort (see the Recall section below).
3. **Tax abatement agreements.** The terms, duration, and value of any tax incentive offered.

4. **Water and energy projections.** Any documents the developer submitted about water consumption or electricity demand.
5. **Economic impact studies.** Any fiscal or economic analysis the locality relied on.

3.4.2 *How to File*

Write a letter or email to your county or city clerk. Cite your state's public records law by name. Be specific about what you want. Set a deadline—most states require a response within five to ten business days.

You do not need a lawyer to file a public records request. No explanation is required for why you want the records. You do not need to say you are investigating a data center. Just ask for the documents.

If the government delays or denies your request, push back. Many states impose penalties for late responses. Contact your state's press association or open government hotline—many offer free legal help for access disputes.

If officials quote you excessive fees, push back—most state laws limit charges to the actual cost of production. Ask for an itemized breakdown and narrow your request if needed.

See Appendix B for a sample public records request letter you can adapt.

3.4.3 *What to Do with the Records*

When the records arrive, look for three things:

Timeline. How long did officials know about the project before the public found out? If the NDA was signed a year ago and the announcement came last month, that is a year of secret negotiations.

Terms. What did the developer promise in private that differs from what they said in public? Internal emails sometimes reveal commitments that did not make it into the official application.

Influence. Did the economic development office lobby the planning board on the developer's behalf? Did the developer suggest specific language for the zoning amendment? These details matter at hearings and in the press.

3.5   GOING TO THE HEARING

Public hearings are your formal chance to influence the decision. Everything you say becomes part of the official record.

3.5.1   Before the Hearing

Get the application. Call the planning office and ask for the conditional use permit application, the site plan, and any studies the developer submitted. These are public documents. Read them before the hearing.

Find the comment deadline. Written comments submitted before the deadline carry the same legal weight as spoken testimony. If the decision is later challenged in court, the judge reviews the written record—not just what was said at the podium.

Talk to your neighbors. Five residents who show up together are more effective than one person speaking alone. Plan your comments so you cover different topics—one person on noise, one on water, one on traffic, one on tax abatements. Splitting topics avoids overlap and shows the board that the pushback is organized and broad, not a single complaint.

3.5.2   At the Hearing

Arrive 30 minutes early. Sign up to speak. Most hearings give each speaker two to three minutes.

Speak to the decision-makers, not to the audience. State your name and address. Focus on one or two specific points. Cite specific numbers from the application.

Avoid vague complaints. "This project will ruin our community" is less effective than a specific claim. Try: "The application projects 55 decibels at the property line—a running dishwasher, 24 hours a day—and the nearest home is 200 feet away."

Ask specific questions. "What is the clawback provision if the developer does not create the promised jobs?" "Who pays for the grid upgrades—ratepayers or the developer?" "What is the water source, and what happens in a drought year?"

The board may not answer your questions at the hearing. That is fine. The questions are now on the record.

Checklist: Before the Hearing

1. Get the application from the planning office. Read the site plan, noise study, water projections, and traffic study.
2. Write your comments around one or two points. Use numbers from the application.
3. Coordinate with neighbors so each speaker covers a different topic.
4. Submit written comments before the deadline, even if you plan to speak.
5. Arrive 30 minutes early. Sign up to speak. Bring copies for the clerk.

3.5.3 *After the Hearing*

After the hearing, the planning commission makes a recommendation to the governing body—your city council or board of supervisors. The governing body votes.

If the vote is yes, get the written conditions of approval. Read every condition. Set calendar reminders for every deadline. If the developer violates a condition—exceeds the noise limit, skips a water monitoring report, fails to post a decommissioning bond—file a complaint with the planning office immediately. If the planning office does not act, in some states you may have standing to enforce the conditions yourself. Ask a local land-use attorney (see Chapter 6).

Standing   The legal right to bring a case or participate in a proceeding. You usually have standing if a decision directly affects you— for example, you live near the project site.

If the vote is yes with weak conditions, you can appeal if the governing body ignored its own zoning code or failed to consider material evidence. You can file a nuisance claim (see Chapter 6). And you can organize for the next election (see below).

If the vote is no, the developer may appeal to a court. A strong record of detailed testimony, specific data, and unanswered questions makes the denial easier to defend. A board that denies a permit with 50 written comments, 20 speakers, and a water impact analysis is much harder to overturn than one that acts without findings. Build the record as if the case is going to court. It might.

Check your local code for the appeal window—often as short as 10 to 30 days. Some jurisdictions allow an appeal of the planning board's decision to the governing body or a board of zoning appeals.

3.5.4 Building the Record

Everything you submit goes into the official record: letters, testimony, questions, data. A judge who later reviews a permit challenge will see exactly what was— and was not—said.

A strong record includes:

- Written testimony from residents about noise, traffic, water, and property value concerns.
- Your own data that counters the builder's claims—if the builder says "minimal noise," include the decibel ratings for the gear they plan to install.
- Questions the board failed to answer. Silence is on the record.
- Expert input from an engineer, a water specialist, or a home appraiser. Independent analysis carries weight.

Your state university extension office or environmental studies program may have water, noise, or environmental experts willing to testify at a hearing. Some law schools run environmental law clinics that offer free help to communities facing development disputes. Ask.

3.6 Open Meetings and Transparency

If your local government is making data center decisions behind closed doors, you may have a legal claim.

Every state has an open meetings law that requires public bodies to do business in the open, with advance notice and a chance for public comment. Closed sessions are allowed for a short list of topics—usually staff matters, lawsuits, and real estate deals.

Data center deals stretch those limits. A closed session to discuss selling a county-owned parcel may be legal. A closed session to discuss zoning changes, tax breaks, or infrastructure the county will build is likely not. If the agenda says "economic development" with no further detail, that is a red flag.

NDAs compound the problem. In Bessemer, Alabama, residents could not learn basic facts about a proposed data center because city officials had signed NDAs. In Saline Township, Michigan, a resident challenged a data center settlement as a violation of the Open Meetings Act. A judge disagreed, ruling there had been a public comment period and the challenge was filed past the 30-day deadline. NDAs between public officials and private companies are themselves public records in most states—file a records request for the agreement itself.

Officials: you can push back on NDAs. An Ohio state representative who served 11 years on local boards put it simply: "I never signed an NDA, and I never would. Secrecy breeds distrust amongst the taxpayers." If you are asked to sign one, demand three changes before you agree. Set a 180-day expiration date. Require that all project details become public at least 90 days before any vote. Add a carve-out stating the NDA does not override your state's open records law.

Pima County, Arizona, adopted all three after a supervisor discovered he was under an NDA he did not know he had signed. In Virginia, a judge ruled that a water authority could not hide Google's data center water use behind a confidentiality agreement, calling water "a resource too precious" to keep secret.

The developer needs your approval more than you need their secrecy. You can say no.

If you believe decisions are being made in secret:

1. Request meeting agendas and minutes for all closed sessions.
2. File a complaint with your state attorney general's open government hotline.
3. Contact your local newspaper—reporters have standing to challenge closed meetings in court.

3.7 WHEN OFFICIALS WON'T LISTEN

Sometimes the board has already made up its mind. Sometimes the economic development office recruited the project and the officials feel committed. Sometimes the developer's lawyers are more persuasive than your testimony.

You are not out of options.

3.7.1 Elections

Planning board members, county supervisors, and city council members all stand for election. In many towns, these races draw fewer than 2,000 votes. A motivated group of residents can change the makeup of a board. Data center opposition is not a partisan issue—both Republican and Democratic officials have won on it. For how to organize around an election, see Chapter 9.

3.7.2 Recall

If an election is too far away, some states allow recall of local officials. Recall rules vary widely by state and town. Signature thresholds can be high—often 25% or more of registered voters within a short time period. Check your state and local rules before starting.

In Festus, Missouri, residents launched a recall effort against four council members and the mayor after the city council voted to annex and rezone land for a data center campus. Emails obtained through public records requests showed that officials had been talking to the developer for months before telling residents. In Port Washington, Wisconsin, residents are trying to recall the mayor over a $15 billion data center proposal.

Recall is hard—it requires collecting thousands of signatures in weeks. But the threat changes how officials behave. Even an unsuccessful petition sends a message. Officials who know a recall is possible are more likely to hold public hearings and answer questions on the record.

3.7.3 Referenda

A referendum lets voters override a decision made by their elected officials. Some states allow referenda on zoning decisions. Others do not. Check your state's laws before investing time in signatures.

In Festus, Missouri, more than 1,400 residents signed a petition demanding a special election on whether to ban large-scale data centers. Only about 1,000 people had voted in the last mayoral election.

In Marana, Arizona, a referendum petition was rejected on a technicality—missing legal descriptions—after residents collected 2,800 signatures (see Chapter 1). The lesson: get a lawyer before you start collecting signatures. The rules are specific and unforgiving.

Before launching a recall or referendum, talk to a local attorney. Petition errors can invalidate months of work: missing legal descriptions, wrong formatting, or not enough signatures.

> ### ✔ What You Can Do
>
> **Local government action plan:**
> 1. **Check the zoning code.** Are data centers allowed by right in any zone? If yes, push for a zoning text amendment to require conditional use permits. This is the single most important change.
> 2. **Push for a moratorium.** Ask your board to pause data center applications while the community studies the impacts and updates its zoning rules. Bring the White County, Indiana, example.
> 3. **File public records requests.** Ask for NDAs, developer correspondence, tax abatement terms, and economic impact studies. You have a legal right to these documents.
> 4. **Attend the hearing.** Show up early, sign up to speak, and focus on specific numbers from the application. Written comments count too.
> 5. **Plan for the next election.** If the board approves a project you opposed, start organizing for the next election now. Local races are small enough to win with a few hundred motivated voters.

CHAPTER FOUR

Fight at the Statehouse

In January 2026, a Virginia resident opened her electric bill and found a new charge. Dominion Energy had raised the base rate by $11.24 per month. The State Corporation Commission had approved the increase to help pay for grid upgrades driven by data center growth in Northern Virginia.

Her county does not have a data center. She pays anyway.

If your fight is about electric bills, water permits, or tax breaks that come from the state, this chapter is where you start.

State government touches data centers at every turn. The utility commission sets the rates. The legislature writes the tax breaks. The environmental agency issues the air and water permits.

The attorney general can intervene in rate cases and challenge deals that harm consumers. And the governor signs or vetoes the legislation that makes the rules.

Here is how to use each one.

4.1 Your Electric Bill Goes to the Statehouse

Local governments approve the building. State utility commissions decide who pays for the power. Here is how that process works and where you can step in.

4.1.1 How Rate Cases Work

Your state has a public utility commission (PUC) or public service commission (PSC). The PUC sets the rates your electric company can charge. When the utility needs more money to build a power plant, upgrade lines, or connect a large new customer, it files a rate case.

A rate case is a legal proceeding. The utility asks for a rate increase. Other parties can file objections: consumer advocates, business groups, green organizations. The commission holds hearings, reviews the evidence, and issues an order.

You can take part. Most commissions accept written comments from the public. Some hold public hearings where residents can testify. In many states, the attorney general's office speaks for ratepayers and will hear your concerns.

4.1.2 The Cost-Shift Fight

The central question in every data center rate case is the same: who pays for the grid upgrades that data centers need?

If the utility builds a new power plant to serve a data center, the cost goes into the "rate base."

Rate base	The total value of a utility's power plants, wires, and equipment that regulators let it earn a profit on. When something goes into the rate base, every customer helps pay for it through their monthly bill.

That cost is then spread across all customers. You pay a share—even if the power plant was built for a single data center.

Rate base charges show up on your monthly bill, but they are not the only cost that gets passed through. The cost shift is not a theory. Chapter 2 showed the numbers: data center demand drove a near-tenfold price spike in PJM's 2025/2026 capacity auction, adding billions in costs to household bills across 13 states.

A capacity auction is where power companies bid to supply electricity for a future period. The winning price gets added to every customer's bill. When data centers drive up demand, auction prices rise and everyone pays more.

4.1.3 The New Rate Classes

Rate base charges and capacity auction costs both land on your bill—but states have started pushing those costs back onto data centers. At least 34 states now have some form of large-load tariff to stop cost-shifting from data centers to other customers.

Michigan set the benchmark. When the Public Service Commission approved the DTE-Oracle/OpenAI contract, it attached the strongest conditions in the country:

- 19-year contracts with 80% minimum billing—the data center pays for 80% of its reserved capacity even if it uses less.
- Load-shed priority: data centers must reduce power before residential customers during grid emergencies.
- Developer-funded energy storage: the data center must fund construction of battery storage to offset its grid impact.

If the data center uses less power than projected, it still pays. If the grid runs short, the data center cuts first. If the project strains the system, the developer pays for the fix.

Virginia created its own large-load rate class (GS-5) with 14-year contracts and 85% minimum billing. Georgia required that large-load customers put "downward pressure of at least $8.50 per month" on a typical home electric bill. Other states are adopting similar rules—search your state PUC's website for "large-load tariff" or "data center rate class."

Ask your utility commission: does your state have a large-load tariff? If it does, ask whether the terms include minimum billing, load-shed priority, and developer-funded infrastructure. Michigan's conditions are the benchmark.

4.1.4 *Behind-the-Meter Power*

Some data centers try to bypass the grid entirely.

Behind-the-Meter	A "behind-the-meter" arrangement connects a data center directly to a power plant, skipping the public grid. The data center buys electricity straight from the generator. Think of it as a private pipeline for power.

Behind-the-meter sounds like it would spare ratepayers. It often does not. The primary concern is co-location—when a data center taps into an existing power plant that was already counted in the grid's reliability planning. When that capacity goes to a data center, other customers lose the benefit. New behind-the-meter generation raises a different problem: it may never be available to the grid at all, leaving the system short during emergencies.

Behind-the-meter arrangements do not protect your rates. Push your utility commission to address them in its rules.

4.1.5   *The Capacity Auction Problem*

PJM runs the regional power grid for 13 states and the District of Columbia. In the 2027/2028 capacity auction, prices hit the maximum cap for the second year in a row. Data center demand accounted for 40% of the $16.4 billion in total auction costs. Check if your utility participates in PJM at https://www. pjm.com. See Chapter 5 for how to participate in FERC proceedings about these auctions.

Your state utility commission controls how those costs are distributed. The commission can require data centers to pay for their own capacity through the large-load tariff—a faster fix than waiting for FERC to change the rules.

4.1.6   *How to Get Involved in a Rate Case*

No law degree is required. Rate cases are designed to allow public participation. Commissioners are regulators, not judges—they expect to hear from the people whose bills they are setting.

Find the docket. Search your state PUC's website for open cases involving your utility. The case will have a docket number. Write it down—you will need it for every filing. If you cannot find the case, call the commission's public information office and ask.

File public comments. Most commissions have an online portal or accept comments by mail. State your name and address, cite the docket number, and explain how the rate increase affects you. Be specific: "My electric bill has risen from $120 to $165 per month over the past two years. I am on a fixed income. I want to know how much of this increase comes from data center load growth."

In Idaho, a retiree testified that the utility's 9.7% rate increase conflicted with her 2.8% Social Security adjustment. A county commissioner told the commission that the costs of growth "weren't being fairly distributed." Their testimony put data center cost-shifting on the public record in a state where few people had connected the dots.

Commissioners read public comments. They do not read most of them in full, but their staff counts them. Volume matters. If 500 ratepayers file comments about data center cost-shifting, the commission notices.

Attend public hearings. Some rate cases include public comment sessions, often held in the evening at locations around the service territory. These are your chance to speak directly to the commissioners. Be specific, cite numbers, focus on impact.

Contact the consumer advocate. Many states have a public advocate or consumer counsel who speaks for ratepayers in utility cases. The consumer advocate's office has lawyers and analysts who can amplify your concerns. Search for "[your state] consumer advocate utility" or "[your state] public counsel," or check the National Association of State Utility Consumer Advocates (NA-SUCA) directory at https://www.nasuca.org. The consumer advocate can challenge the utility's cost allocation—arguing that data center grid upgrades should be charged to data centers, not to all customers.

Intervene formally. In most states, any person or organization can file to intervene in a rate case. Intervening gives you the right to submit evidence, cross-examine witnesses, and receive all filings. It is more work than filing comments. But if you have a group of organized residents, intervention lets you participate as a full party. Environmental groups and consumer organizations often intervene and may welcome additional participants.

Track the timeline. Rate cases move on a schedule. Miss a deadline and you lose your chance. When you find the docket, write down every deadline and set reminders.

> **☞ *What This Means for You***
>
> A rate case is where the real money decisions happen. The zoning hearing determined where the building goes. The rate case determines who pays for the electricity. If you care about your electric bill, this is the fight that matters.

Michigan showed what an attorney general can do. DTE Energy sought approval for a 1.4-gigawatt data center contract. Attorney General Dana Nessel demanded a formal public hearing and challenged the approval when DTE failed to provide written guarantees. Her office is still fighting. See the Attorney General section below for how to push your AG to take similar action.

4.2 TAX BREAK REFORM

Chapter 2 laid out the numbers: states lose 50 to 70 cents on every dollar they spend on data center tax breaks. Every state that has audited its program has found a net loss. Those losses are not abstract. Every dollar in foregone revenue is a dollar your community has to raise from other sources—or go without.

4.2.1 What to Push For

If your state offers data center tax breaks, push for reform:

1. Disclosure. Only 11 states disclose which companies get data center breaks. You cannot evaluate a program you cannot see.

You can start by looking up what is already public. Good Jobs First runs a Subsidy Tracker at https://subsidytracker.goodjobsfirst.org. Search by your state to see which companies received breaks, how much they got, and what they promised. Bring those numbers to hearings.

Your lawmakers can fix this with a short bill. Require annual public reporting of every tax break recipient, the amount foregone, the jobs promised, and the jobs actually created.

2. Clawback provisions. If the developer does not meet its job or investment promises, the tax break should shrink or end. Most existing clawbacks are too weak to matter. About 75% of state programs have some form of penalty, but most give enforcement discretion to the same officials who approved the deal. Good Jobs First recommends a 5% per year clawback for each year job levels are not met, with mandatory enforcement—not discretionary.

3. Sunset clauses. No tax break should last 50 years. Indiana's 50-year exemption means the state is committing to forgone revenue for half a century based on today's technology and today's projections. Build in 5-year review dates. If the program is working, renew it. If not, let it expire.

4. Independent cost-benefit analysis. Require the state to study the return on investment every five years, using independent analysts—not consultants hired by the developer. Virginia, Georgia, and Washington all found that the programs cost more than they returned. The problem is that most states have never studied it at all.

5. Local opt-out. Some state programs force local governments to participate. The state grants the exemption, and the county or school district loses the property tax revenue. Push for a local opt-out that lets communities decide whether to participate. Indiana legislators have proposed letting counties opt out of a 1% property tax PILOT (payment in lieu of taxes) and require a higher rate. Your state should allow the same.

Data center tax incentives follow a predictable pattern: a state passes generous breaks, auditors later discover the cost exceeds projections and the jobs fell short, and lawmakers propose reform. Find where your state is in this cycle. If auditors have already flagged problems, use their reports. If not, ask your state legislative audit office to study the program. The request alone puts the issue on the agenda.

States are already moving. Georgia's legislature voted to suspend its exemption in 2024. The governor vetoed it, but the debate is on the record. Indiana offers 50-year incentives for investments over $750 million—but data center buildings have a 20-year lifespan. The incentive outlasts the building.

Illinois shows what a freeze looks like. In February 2026, Governor J.B. Pritzker announced a two-year freeze on new data center tax incentives. The program's cost had grown from $10 million in 2020 to $370 million in 2023—a 3,600% increase in three years. Illinois became the first state to pause its data center incentive program entirely, giving the state time to study whether the program is working. Georgia's auditors found that 70% of data centers would have come without incentives. If data centers keep coming anyway, it proves the tax breaks were never necessary.

See the State Elections section below for how to bring these asks to your state lawmaker.

4.3 WATER

Data center water use is largely secret. Most states do not require data centers to report how much water they consume.

Texas data centers used roughly 25 billion gallons in 2025. Projections range from 29 to 161 billion gallons per year by 2030. Texas has no rule requiring data centers to disclose their water use.

Georgia requires permits for groundwater withdrawals over 100,000 gallons per day. A proposed bill, the Data Center Transparency Act, would require public disclosure of water and electricity use.

Indiana has proposed one of the strongest water rules in the country. House Bill 1043 would require state water permits for data centers using more than 10 million gallons per month, with mandated conservation and public reporting.

4.3.1 *What to Ask For*

Ask your state lawmakers to support three measures:

Mandatory water reporting. Data centers should report actual water use on a public schedule. Not projected, not guessed—metered. At least eight states introduced water reporting bills in 2025. Governors in California and Virginia vetoed them. New Jersey's governor issued a conditional veto. The industry has fought water transparency at every level. That resistance tells you the numbers are worth knowing.

Water impact studies. Before a data center is approved, the developer should study the impact on local water supplies. The study should include drought-year scenarios, not just averages. If the facility uses groundwater, the study should model the impact on neighboring wells.

In Newton County, Georgia, Beverly and Jeff Morris live 1,000 feet from a Meta data center. After the facility opened, their well went dry. Their dishwasher, washing machine, and toilet all stopped working. They spent $5,000 on repairs and still cannot afford to replace the well. Three of their neighbors had the same problem.

In Virginia, industrial pumping has created "cones of depression" in the Potomac Aquifer that threaten private wells. When the aquifer drops, wells go dry.

In northeast Pennsylvania, residents organized in early 2026 over fears that proposed data centers would deplete local water resources. Where data centers pay bulk commercial rates while residents pay higher retail rates, the disparity fuels public anger—and it is excellent material for public testimony.

Find out how much water your local data center uses. File a public records request with your municipal water authority for the data center's water allocation and actual consumption. If the contract is between the developer and a private water company, your state's environmental agency may have the withdrawal permit on file.

Permits for large withdrawals. If your state does not require water permits for data center volumes, it should. A facility using 10 million gallons per month is an industrial water consumer, not a commercial office building.

Drought-year protections. State law should require drought-year curtailment clauses in every large industrial water contract. Right now, most data center agreements lock in a fixed daily volume with no reduction trigger. Your legislators can fix that. Draft bills should mandate tiered pricing for industrial users above a threshold, say 500,000 gallons per month, and automatic cutbacks that match residential conservation orders. Oregon and Colorado already apply curtailment rules to large agricultural users. The same principle works for data centers.

If your governor has vetoed a water disclosure bill, that veto is an issue in the next election. Document it. Share it with your coalition. Ask candidates for governor whether they would sign the same bill. Water disclosure bills that were dead under one governor may pass under the next.

4.3.2 *Water Rights by State*

Water law varies by state and may give you a legal claim if a data center's pumping damages your well or lowers your water table. Ask a water rights attorney, or see Chapter 6 for details on property-based claims.

4.4 ENVIRONMENTAL REVIEW

About 16 states have laws like the federal NEPA that require environmental review of major projects. California, Washington, New York, and Minnesota have the strongest.

In most states, data centers slip through. They are built on private land with private money. They do not trigger the review that a highway or a dam would.

Two openings exist:

Air quality permits. Backup diesel generators need air permits in most states. These permits limit how many hours the generators can run and how much they can pollute. If the data center has dozens of generators, the total emissions may trigger a tougher review.

Local land use. If the project requires a conditional use permit (see Chapter 3), the local review may include an environmental check. In states with strong review laws, the local permit can trigger a full environmental impact study.

If your state has a "little NEPA" or state environmental policy act, find out what triggers it. In many states, a discretionary permit is the trigger: a conditional use permit or a rezoning. If data centers are built by right, there is no permit decision, and no review. That is another reason to push for conditional use permits at the local level (see Chapter 3). A single zoning change can trigger a full review process.

In Minnesota, Monticello completed a joint workshop between its Planning Commission and City Council in December 2024 before allowing any data center development. The city amended its long-range plan to limit data centers to Light Industrial Park areas and is conducting a full Alternative Urban Areawide environmental review. That is a model for communities in states with environmental review laws.

If your state does not have a "little NEPA," push for one. At minimum, push for a rule requiring an environmental impact study before any data center over 100,000 square feet can be permitted. The study should cover noise, water, air quality, traffic, and cumulative effects from nearby facilities. It should be paid for by the developer, reviewed by the state, and open to public comment.

4.4.1 *Air Quality*

Backup diesel generators need air permits from your state environmental agency. A large campus with 20 or 30 generators may produce enough pollution together to require a New Source Review (NSR) permit under the Clean Air Act.

Air permitting is where state and federal tools overlap. Your state issues the permit. The EPA sets the standards. If your state agency is slow to enforce, the EPA regional office can intervene.

In Mississippi, xAI installed gas turbines at its Southaven data center without air permits—and the state initially did not act. Environmental groups threatened a Clean Air Act citizen suit, which forced compliance. See Chapter 5 for how citizen suits work and how to use federal enforcement tools.

4.5 YOUR ATTORNEY GENERAL

Your state attorney general can intervene in rate cases, investigate NDAs between developers and local officials, and challenge projects that violate state law. Attorneys general are elected in 43 states. They respond to voters. Michigan's Dana Nessel is the only AG who has used these tools on a data center case so far. That means the field is wide open.

Write to your attorney general's office. Ten letters from the same county start a conversation. Most AGs have a consumer protection hotline and an open government division. You are not asking them to file a lawsuit tomorrow. You are building a record that makes the next action possible.

4.6 STATE ELECTIONS

4.6.1 *Your Utility Commission*

Ten states elect their PUC or PSC commissioners. In November 2026, voters in nine states will choose 14 commissioners. These are the people who decide whether data center costs land on your electric bill.

These races are usually quiet. Few voters know who their utility commissioner is. That makes them winnable for organized groups with a clear message.

If your state elects its commissioners, find out when the next race is. Ask candidates one question: who should pay for data center grid upgrades—the data center, or everyone else?

4.6.2 *Your State Lawmakers*

Every state lawmaker votes on tax break programs, moratorium authority, and utility rules. In 2025, legislators in all 50 states considered at least 238 data center-related bills. More than 40 became law. Data centers are on every statehouse agenda.

Before you call, find out what is already moving. Search your state legislature's website for bills containing "data center." Most legislatures have a free bill-search tool and offer email alerts when a bill's status changes. Data Center Watch and Food & Water Watch publish legislative trackers that sort bills by state.

Knowing what is in play makes your call specific. "I am calling to ask the senator to co-sponsor House Bill 1043" works better than "I am worried about data centers."

Find your state representative and senator. Tell them what is happening in your community. Ask for the things this chapter covers: rate protection, tax transparency, water disclosure, and environmental review.

Bring a one-page summary of the problem. Include your electric bill, the name of the data center developer in your area, and the specific bills you want the lawmaker to sponsor or support. The most effective approach: bring a specific bill number from another state. Indiana's water permit bill, Illinois's incentive pause, and Michigan's ratepayer protections are all models. Legislators are more comfortable voting for something that already exists elsewhere.

In DeForest, Wisconsin, two residents started a Facebook group called "No Data Center in DeForest" after learning that QTS-Blackstone was planning a $12 billion campus on farmland. The group grew to 4,000 followers in a village of 10,000. A state senator who received a flood of calls from the district introduced a Data Center Accountability Act requiring water and energy transparency. On February 3, 2026, the village board voted unanimously against the project.

One phone call matters. Ten phone calls from the same district change votes. A hundred letters from the same county change bills.

In Florida, Governor DeSantis proposed legislation to let local governments reject data centers, ban utility cost pass-throughs, and prevent construction on agricultural land. South Dakota's Senate passed a "Data Center Bill of Rights" unanimously. The bill requires data centers to pay their own electricity costs and bars the state from overruling local authority on data center rules. The opposition crosses party lines because the costs do.

State lawmakers also control whether local governments have the power to impose moratoria. In some states, the legislature must grant moratorium authority. In others, home rule gives localities the power already. If your local government says it cannot pause data center permits, ask your state representative whether that is true—and if it is, ask for a bill to fix it.

4.6.3 *The Governor*

Your governor signs or vetoes legislation. If your governor has vetoed data center reform bills, that veto is an issue in the next election. In Virginia, New Jersey, and Georgia, candidates who made data center costs a campaign issue won statewide races (see Chapter 10 for details). The issue crosses party lines because the costs affect everyone: higher bills, less water, more noise.

Write to your governor. Ask them to support the specific measures in this chapter. If they will not, ask the candidates running to replace them.

☑ What You Can Do

State-level action plan:

1. **Find your utility docket.** Search your state PUC's website for rate cases involving your utility. Write down the docket number and the public comment deadline.

2. **File comments.** Tell the commission how electricity cost increases affect your household. Cite the docket number. Ask who pays for data center grid upgrades.

3. **Contact the consumer advocate.** Your state likely has a public counsel or consumer advocate who speaks for ratepayers. Ask them to review data center cost allocation in your utility's rate case.

4. **Write your state lawmakers.** Ask for three things: mandatory water reporting for data centers, disclosure of tax break recipients, and clawback provisions for unmet job promises.

5. **Check your AG.** Has your state attorney general taken any position on data center utility costs? If not, ask them to. A letter from a voter starts a file.

Fight in Washington

In April 2025, a utility company filed the first of two federal lawsuits against more than 300 Maryland landowners. The company wanted to build a 67-mile, $424 million transmission line through Baltimore, Carroll, and Frederick Counties. The line would destroy over 1,200 acres of farmland to carry electricity from Pennsylvania to Northern Virginia—to power data centers.

The farmers had refused to let surveyors onto their property. The company asked a federal judge to send in U.S. marshals.

Federal tools cut both ways. The federal government can help communities fight data centers. It can also help data centers fight communities. The following sections explain how to tell the difference—and where to intervene.

Federal tools are slower and harder to use than local ones. But they offer something no local tool can: they apply across state lines and can override state decisions. They give you access to courts and federal agencies that are not controlled by local politics.

Federal environmental law is dense. This chapter covers the parts that matter for data center fights—not legal advice, but enough to know what tools exist and when to call a lawyer.

5.1 NEPA: The National Environmental Policy Act

NEPA is the federal law that requires the government to study the environmental impact of major actions before they happen. It applies when a federal agency issues a permit, gives funding, or takes a "major federal action" that affects people or the land.

Most data centers do not trigger NEPA directly. They are private projects on private land. But some do—if the project requires a federal permit (like a 404 wetlands permit), receives federal funding (like a DOE loan or grant), or uses federal land.

If NEPA applies, the agency must prepare either an environmental assessment (EA) or a full environmental impact statement (EIS). Both require public comment. An EIS is the stronger tool: it requires a detailed look at other options, combined impacts, and steps to reduce harm.

5.1.1 The Executive Order Threat

If a data center project in your community requires a federal permit, ask the federal agency in writing whether it will conduct an environmental review. Do not assume a NEPA review will happen on its own.

In July 2025, President Trump signed an executive order aimed at speeding up data center construction. The order told agencies to create "categorical exclusions" for AI data centers over 100 megawatts—meaning the project skips review entirely. It also stated that projects with less than 50% federal funding should be presumed not to be a major federal action. If this becomes policy, many data centers would skip NEPA review even when they get federal permits.

The order is being challenged. Groups like Earthjustice and the Sierra Club are tracking rule changes from the Army Corps and the White House Council on Environmental Quality. If the agency says no review is needed, ask for a written explanation. That letter becomes evidence if you challenge the decision in court.

5.1.2 How to Use NEPA

If the project triggers NEPA, you have several opportunities to participate.

Scoping. Before the agency prepares the environmental review, it holds a scoping period. Submit written comments listing what you want studied: water use, air quality, combined impacts from nearby sites, harm to wildlife. The more specific your comments, the harder they are to ignore.

Draft review. When the agency publishes a draft Environmental Assessment or Environmental Impact Statement, a public comment period follows.

The window varies—check the Federal Register notice for the exact deadline. Read the draft and look for gaps.

Did the agency study water impacts? Did it look at the combined effect of all data centers in the area? Did it weigh other sites for the project?

Final challenge. If the agency issues a "Finding of No Significant Impact" (FONSI) and you believe the review was lacking, that ruling can be challenged in federal court. Groups like Earthjustice and the Sierra Club regularly file these challenges.

NEPA is slow. An EIS can take two or more years. But that delay is itself a tool. A project stuck in environmental review cannot break ground.

5.1.3 Cumulative Impacts

One data center may not seem like a major federal action. But what about ten data centers in the same county? Twenty data centers on the same power grid? A hundred data centers drawing from the same aquifer?

Aquifer	An underground layer of rock or sand that holds water, like a natural reservoir beneath your feet. Wells pump water up from aquifers. Heavy pumping in one spot can lower the water level for everyone nearby.

NEPA requires agencies to consider cumulative impacts. That means the combined effect of a proposed project plus other past, present, and likely future projects in the same area. If your area already has data centers and more are proposed, the cumulative impact on water, air quality, and the power grid may be far larger than any single project.

Raise cumulative impacts in every comment you file. Name the other data centers in the area. Cite their combined water use, their combined generator emissions, their combined electricity demand. A single facility may look manageable. The full picture may not.

5.2 THE CLEAN WATER ACT

Section 404 of the Clean Water Act is the strongest federal tool available to most communities. It requires a permit from the Army Corps of Engineers before anyone fills or disturbs wetlands, streams, or other U.S. waters.

Data center construction often involves filling wetlands. Large campuses are built on hundreds of acres. If even a fraction of that land includes wetlands, streams, or waterways, the developer needs a 404 permit. That permit requires public notice and a comment period.

5.2.1 *How to Use It*

Step 1: Check for wetlands. Go to the National Wetlands Inventory at the U.S. Fish and Wildlife Service website. Enter the address or coordinates of the project site. The map will show any cataloged wetlands. Not all wetlands are mapped—a field survey may reveal more.

Step 2: Watch for the permit application. The Army Corps maintains a public database of permit applications by district. Search your district's website for "public notices." If a 404 application has been filed, the public notice will include a comment period. Deadlines vary by district—check the notice for the exact date.

Step 3: Submit comments. Explain how the project will affect local waterways, wildlife habitat, and water quality. Name the harms: lost acres of wetland, ruined stream miles, dirty water downstream. The Army Corps must consider your comments before issuing the permit.

Step 4: Challenge the permit. If the permit is granted and you believe the process was flawed, you can challenge it in federal court. In Prince William County, Virginia, residents urged the Army Corps to deny a 404 permit for a data center project. The project would fill four acres of forested wetlands and destroy nearly three-quarters of a mile of streams. In a separate Prince William County case, a state court voided the rezoning for the Digital Gateway data center campus. The 404 permit for the wetlands project is still pending.

Section 404 is powerful because it applies no matter what local or state government decides. A county can approve a rezoning. A state can grant a water permit. But if the project fills wetlands without a 404 permit, federal law still applies. That is why federal tools are a backstop for your local fight.

> **◉ Tip**
>
> Not all wetlands appear on the National Wetlands Inventory maps. If the project site looks flat, poorly drained, or has standing water in spring, request a formal wetlands delineation from the Army Corps. The developer may have avoided mapping wetlands to skip the permit process. A field survey by a qualified wetland scientist can identify areas the maps miss.

5.2.2   *The Endangered Species Act*

If the project site is home to a threatened or endangered species, the Endangered Species Act (ESA) adds another layer of protection. The developer must consult with the U.S. Fish and Wildlife Service before proceeding.

In Mingo County, West Virginia, 10 residents filed a federal lawsuit in December 2025 against TransGas Development Systems and three federal agencies, citing ESA, Clean Water Act, and NEPA violations. At a state hearing, a grandmother who had lived in the area her entire life said: "They are only putting the dollar before our health and our lives." The project would pair two gas-burning power plants with two data centers, generating more than 200 tons of regulated air pollutants per year in an Appalachian watershed with endangered species.

You can check whether any listed species live in your area using the Fish and Wildlife Service's online database. If the project site overlaps with critical habitat, flag it in your comments on any federal permit application. If you find a listed species, file a written request with Fish and Wildlife asking for a formal consultation on the project.

5.3   FERC AND THE POWER GRID

The Federal Energy Regulatory Commission (FERC) does not regulate data centers directly. It regulates the transmission lines and wholesale electricity markets that serve them. If your electric bill is going up because of data centers, FERC is part of the reason.

5.3.1   *How Data Center Demand Raises Your Bill*

PJM's capacity auctions set electricity prices for 13 states and 67 million people. In the 2027/2028 auction, data center demand accounted for 40% of the $16.4

billion in total costs—and prices hit the maximum cap for the second year in a row. You pay for that through your electric bill, whether or not you live near a data center.

The Department of Energy has directed FERC to create new rules for connecting large customers (over 20 megawatts) to the grid. State utility leaders have pushed back, saying this would take power away from states and hurt ratepayers. Some data centers draw power directly from a plant, bypassing the public grid—so-called "behind the meter" deals. FERC rejected PJM's proposed tariff for co-located load as "unjust and unreasonable" and ordered new rules. The proceeding is ongoing.

5.3.2 *How to Get Involved*

FERC proceedings are open to the public. Any person or group can file comments on proposed rules. You can also join as an "intervenor" in specific cases, which gives you the right to submit evidence and receive filings.

PJM covers 13 states plus D.C. If you live in any of them, these proceedings affect your electric bill. File a comment. Tell FERC how data center costs are hitting your household.

5.3.3 *How to File a FERC Comment*

Filing a comment with FERC is free. Go to the FERC website and search for the docket number of the proceeding. Click "eComment" or "eFiling" depending on whether you are an individual or an organization.

Write a short letter—one page is enough. State your name, your address, and the docket number. Explain how the issue affects you. If your electric bill has gone up, say by how much. If a transmission line is proposed near your property, describe the impact.

FERC is a technical agency. Commissioners are used to hearing from lawyers and lobbyists. A comment from a regular person who says "my electricity bill went up $40 this month because of data center costs" stands out. File one. Ask ten neighbors to file too.

5.3.4 *Transmission Lines*

Transmission lines affect communities that may never see a data center. A farmer 50 miles from the nearest server room loses land to a tower. At least a dozen high-voltage lines have been proposed in PJM states since 2024, all driven by data center demand.

Find out if a line is planned near you. PJM publishes its Regional Transmission Expansion Plan online. Search it for lines near your community.

Comment on the proposal. When a utility files to build a transmission line, it needs a certificate of public convenience and necessity from the state. That proceeding is open to public comment. If the line runs through your community, you have standing to object. If the line crosses wetlands, a Section 404 permit is also required.

Eminent domain	The government's power to take private land for public use, even if the owner does not want to sell. The government must pay, but the owner cannot refuse. Utilities sometimes use this power for transmission lines that serve data centers.

If the utility needs your land and you will not sell, it can seek eminent domain. The Maryland farmers in the opening of this chapter refused surveyors and forced the utility into federal court.

Push for stronger protections. Maryland legislators proposed the Protect Maryland Farm Lands Act, which would require a 350% premium over the highest appraised value for any eminent domain taking of agricultural land. That kind of law changes the economics of a transmission line. If your state is seeing new transmission proposals, ask your lawmakers to introduce similar protections.

5.4 DEPARTMENT OF ENERGY

The DOE Loan Programs Office has provided or guaranteed billions of dollars in loans for energy projects, including power plants and transmission lines that serve data centers. If a project receives DOE funding, NEPA applies. The review rule follows the federal dollar.

Check the DOE Loan Programs Office website for announcements, or ask the developer directly whether federal funds are involved. When DOE issues a loan guarantee for a power plant that will serve a data center, you can submit comments during the NEPA review. Ask whether the review considered the data center's water use, the cumulative emissions from backup generators, and the impact on the local power grid.

5.5　The Clean Air Act

Data centers run on grid power most of the time. But they have rows of backup diesel generators that run during outages and monthly testing. Virginia alone has permitted about 8,000 diesel generators for data centers.

Diesel generators put out soot, nitrogen oxides, and sulfur dioxide. A UC Riverside and Caltech study (a preprint not yet peer-reviewed) projected that data center air pollution could cause an estimated 1,300 early deaths per year by 2028. That figure covers both grid power plants and backup generators. The projected yearly health cost: $12 to $21 billion, assuming continued growth.

In Northern Virginia, hundreds of data centers operate within a few miles of each other. No one has fully studied what happens to air quality when thousands of diesel generators run at the same time. That gap in the data is itself a reason to demand a full air quality study before any new site is approved.

5.5.1　What You Can Do

Backup generators need air permits from your state environmental agency. Those permits limit how many hours the generators can run. The federal rule allows up to 100 hours per year for testing.

If the data center has dozens of generators, the combined emissions may trigger a New Source Review (NSR) permit under the Clean Air Act. NSR permits require public notice and comment.

Contact your state air quality agency. Ask whether the data center has an air permit. Ask how many generators are on site. Ask whether the combined emissions trigger NSR.

If multiple data centers are clustered near each other, the combined emissions may be even larger.

That same study put data center-related air pollution at \$6.7 billion in U.S. health costs in 2023. Backup generators alone accounted for \$500 million of that total—and the share is growing as more sites come online. Cite these numbers in your comments.

If the agency is slow to respond, contact the EPA regional office for your state. You can also check the EPA's ECHO database (Enforcement and Compliance History Online) to see whether the facility has already been cited for violations. If it has not been inspected, that itself is worth noting—and worth asking the EPA about. Start with your state air quality agency: ask for the facility's permit file and submit a written request for an inspection.

5.5.2 *Citizen Suits*

The Clean Air Act includes a citizen suit provision. If the government fails to enforce an air quality violation, any person can file a lawsuit to compel enforcement.

The rule: you must give 60 days' written notice to the polluter, the EPA, and the state before filing suit. If the government takes action during those 60 days, you may not need to go to court. The threat of a lawsuit is often enough.

In Mississippi, the NAACP, the Southern Environmental Law Center, and Earthjustice sent notice of intent to sue xAI for operating 27 gas turbines without air permits. The state had not acted. The citizen suit rule gave these groups the legal right to step in where the state had not.

The citizen suit rule is available to you. Anyone can file, not just groups. You do need a lawyer, because filing a citizen suit means following strict rules. Earthjustice and the Southern Environmental Law Center take cases at no cost to communities. See Appendix C for how to contact them.

Federal law also requires agencies to consider whether a project puts an unfair burden on low-income communities or communities already hit hard by pollution. If yours qualifies, that triggers extra review. Use that rule in your comments and legal filings.

5.6 THE CLEAN WATER ACT: SECTION 402

Section 404 covers filling wetlands. Section 402 covers water discharges.

If the data center discharges cooling water, stormwater, or wastewater, it may need a National Pollutant Discharge Elimination System (NPDES) permit under Section 402. These permits set limits on temperature, pH, and pollutant levels.

Data center cooling systems that dump warm water can hurt fish and other water life. Permits set limits on discharge temperature. If the data center discharges to a stream, check whether it has an NPDES permit on your state environmental agency's website. If it does not, report the unpermitted discharge to the agency and to the EPA—put the report in writing so you have a record.

5.7 YOUR MEMBERS OF CONGRESS

Federal legislation on data centers is still early. Bills have been filed but not passed. The most relevant:

The Data Center Transparency Act would require EPA and the Energy Information Administration to collect and publish data on data center energy use, water use, and air quality impacts.

The Protecting Families from AI Data Center Energy Costs Act would require FERC to study how data center costs affect household electric bills and recommend protections.

Senators Warren, Van Hollen, and Blumenthal have opened a formal investigation into data center energy costs. They sent letters to Google, Microsoft, Amazon, Meta, CoreWeave, Digital Realty, and Equinix.

None of these bills have passed. But pressure from Congress creates public records, generates news coverage, and signals to regulators that someone is watching. The letters alone forced the companies to hand over documents and answer questions about their energy use.

These probes are not laws. They are fact-finding tools. But what they turn up becomes public. When a senator sends a letter to Google asking how much water its data centers use, Google must respond on the record. That response becomes a document you can cite at your local planning hearing.

A coalition of more than 230 environmental groups petitioned Congress in December 2025 for a national construction moratorium on data centers. A national moratorium is unlikely in today's political climate, but the letter put the issue on the record in Congress.

5.7.1 What to Ask Your Representative

Call your member of Congress. Ask four questions:

1. Where do they stand on data center energy costs?
2. Will they support the Data Center Transparency Act?
3. Will they ask FERC to protect ratepayers from data center cost-shifting?
4. Will they push DOE to set a national data center energy efficiency standard? (Data centers consumed 4.4% of U.S. electricity in 2023 and could reach 6.7 to 12% by 2028.)

A phone call to a congressional office takes five minutes. A staffer logs the call. If enough calls come in on the same topic, the office generates a letter from the member to the relevant agency.

Phone calls are more effective than emails. Ten calls from the same district on the same topic in the same week get the member's attention.

Attend town halls during recess periods. A question asked on the record, in front of other voters, is harder to ignore than a phone call. You can also request a constituent meeting—bring a group of neighbors, your electric bill, and a one-page summary of the project.

Timing matters. Contact your member of Congress when data center bills are moving through committee or when a FERC docket is open for comment. Organizations like Food & Water Watch issue action alerts timed to key votes.

If your member of Congress sits on the Energy and Commerce Committee or the Environment and Public Works Committee, they have direct say over these issues. Ask whether they will request data from the companies building in your community. A letter from a senator to a data center company asking about local impacts gets answered.

5.7.2 The Lobbying Imbalance

The Data Center Coalition nearly tripled its lobbying spending in the third quarter of 2025. The electronics sector spent $226 million on lobbying that year. A new AI trade group hands out talking points to members of Congress and runs local "data center field trips" to make the industry look friendly.

You cannot outspend the industry, but you can outorganize it. A hundred phone calls from voters outweigh a million-dollar lobby push if the calls are clear, personal, and steady. See Chapter 9 for how to organize those calls. When the lobby budget triples, it tells you the industry is paying attention to community opposition.

Data center demand creates impacts far beyond the building site. Transmission lines, substations, solar farms, battery storage facilities, and gas pipelines affect communities that may never see the data center itself. The infrastructure cascade is real: one campus can trigger land-use conflicts across an entire region. Data centers are not the only driver—the broader energy transition also requires new infrastructure—but a single data center project can concentrate years of demand into months.

Federal tools matter here because these supply-chain projects often cross county and state lines, putting them beyond the reach of any single local government.

5.8 WHEN FEDERAL TOOLS ARE WEAK

Federal environmental law is changing. An executive order on data center permitting aims to speed approvals. In 2025, the Supreme Court narrowed the scope of NEPA review. EPA has loosened rules on when construction can begin before air permits are issued. The trend: fewer reviews, faster timelines, and less public input at the federal level.

Federal tools still work. The 404 permit process still requires public comment. FERC proceedings are still open. Air quality permits still apply.

But do not rely on federal tools alone. Combine them with state and local tools from chapters 3 and 4.

Delay is itself a tool—the longer permitting takes, the more time you have to organize locally. Federal filings also create permanent records. A NEPA comment, a FERC filing, or a citizen suit notice survives changes in administration. The records you create today may support action years from now.

> ### ☑ What You Can Do
>
> **Federal action plan:**
>
> 1. **Check for wetlands.** Search the National Wetlands Inventory for the project site. If wetlands are present, watch for a Section 404 permit application from the Army Corps. Submit comments during the public notice period.
>
> 2. **File FERC comments.** If you live in a PJM state, file a comment in the large-load interconnection proceeding. Tell FERC how data center costs are affecting your electric bill.
>
> 3. **Ask about air permits.** Contact your state air quality agency and ask whether the data center has a permit for its backup generators. Ask how many generators are on site and whether the combined emissions trigger New Source Review.
>
> 4. **Call your member of Congress.** Ask where they stand on data center energy costs and the Data Center Transparency Act. One phone call takes five minutes.
>
> 5. **Combine tools.** Federal tools work best in combination with state and local action. File comments at every level of government.

CHAPTER SIX

Fight for Your Property

Stephanie Brookes moved to Loudoun County, Virginia, in 2021. By early 2023, she started hearing a low hum from a data center built near her home. The sound never stopped. It was louder at night, when the rest of the world was quiet. Residents described the noise as a drone hovering above their houses, 24 hours a day.

Other neighbors heard it too. Some described the noise as a freight train, a leaf blower, a propeller. Children had nightmares. One resident said his headboard vibrated. People moved their children's bedrooms to the basement.

Loudoun County had 175 data centers in 2023 and more than 200 by late 2025. The noise comes from cooling fans, chillers, air handlers, and backup generators—all running around the clock. And as of early 2026, no one in that county has received a dollar in compensation.

What follows is about your legal rights as a property owner. When government tools from chapters 3 through 5 are not enough, private law gives you another path. You can sue.

Tort	A legal term for a wrongful act that harms someone, which the harmed person can sue over. Nobody goes to jail—but the person or company responsible may have to pay money for the damage.

None of what follows is legal advice. It explains the tools that exist so you can have an informed conversation with a lawyer.

6.1 NOISE

Noise is the most common complaint from people who live near data centers. It is also the strongest legal claim most neighbors have.

6.1.1 How Loud Is a Data Center?

A data center is not one noise source. It is dozens, all running at once. And unlike a factory that shuts down at night, a data center never stops.

Cooling fans produce up to 90 decibels. Air-cooled chillers hit 100 decibels—as loud as a motorcycle. Rooftop air handlers produce 85 to 100 decibels each, and a large facility may have a dozen. Backup diesel generators reach 100 to 110 decibels during testing or outages.

For comparison, the American Speech-Language-Hearing Association says that sounds at or below 70 decibels are safe. Above 85, hearing damage begins.

The sound does not stay on the property. Low-frequency noise travels farther than higher-pitched sounds. The deep hum that data centers produce passes through walls and windows. One homeowner in Prince William County, Virginia, reported hearing an AWS facility from 600 feet away.

In Prince William County, Virginia, residents along the I-66 corridor gave the sound a name: the Haymarket Hum. Families said it pushed them to the edge. Some sought medical help. Others moved.

6.1.2 Health Effects

Low-frequency noise does not just annoy. It harms.

The health effects documented in medical literature include sleep deprivation, chronic anxiety, hypertension, headaches, dizziness, and impaired focus. Long-term exposure to noise above 85 decibels causes hearing loss.

Children are especially vulnerable. In Loudoun County, families described the effects from the chapter opening—the hum, the nightmares, the children moved to basements.

If you are experiencing health effects from data center noise, see your doctor. Ask for a written record that links your symptoms to the noise exposure. That record is evidence in a legal claim. The sooner you create it, the stronger it is.

6.1.3 *What the Law Says*

Most cities and counties have noise ordinances. They set limits measured at the property line, usually in decibels. Typical residential limits range from 50 to 65 decibels during the day and 45 to 55 decibels at night.

If the data center exceeds those limits, the operator is violating local law. Call your local code enforcement office to file a complaint. Include the date, time, duration, and location of the noise. If you have decibel readings, include those. Ask for a case number and follow up in writing.

In Chicago, residents in the Printer's Row neighborhood filed repeated complaints about fan noise from a Digital Realty data center. The city's health department measured the sound and confirmed it exceeded the noise ordinance. Digital Realty was fined $300.

Three hundred dollars is not much of a deterrent for a company worth billions. That is why code enforcement alone is often not enough.

6.1.4 *Nuisance: The Legal Claim*

Private nuisance is a legal claim that says someone else's use of their property is unreasonably interfering with your use of yours.

To win a nuisance case, you generally need to show six things:

1. You own or have the right to occupy the property.
2. The other party's actions interfere with your use and enjoyment.
3. The interference is substantial, not a minor annoyance.
4. The interference is unreasonable, considering the harm to you weighed against the burden of stopping it.
5. The conduct is intentional or negligent. The operator knows the noise reaches your property and continues anyway.
6. You suffered actual harm.

Courts apply an "ordinary person" test. The question is not whether you are unusually sensitive. The question is whether a typical person in your position would find the interference intolerable.

One defense to watch for: "coming to the nuisance." If the data center was built before you moved in, the developer may argue you chose to live near it. This defense does not always win, but it is stronger when the data center predates the neighborhood. If you already live there when the data center is proposed, this defense is unlikely to apply.

6.1.5 What You Can Win

If a court finds nuisance, it can award several types of relief.

Money damages. If the nuisance is temporary, meaning it can be fixed, you can recover for the loss of use and enjoyment you have already suffered. If the nuisance is permanent, you can recover the lost market value of your property.

An injunction. An injunction is a court order requiring the data center to reduce the noise. The operator might have to install sound barriers, replace equipment, or limit operations during certain hours. An injunction changes behavior. A fine does not.

Medical costs. If the noise caused documented health problems such as sleep loss, anxiety, or hypertension, you may recover those costs too.

No court has yet awarded a large nuisance judgment against a data center for noise. But courts have awarded millions in analogous cases. In Texas, a jury awarded more than $2 million for lost property value caused by noise from a natural gas compressor station. The Texas Supreme Court later ordered a new trial, but the precedent stands. In California, the state supreme court ruled that homeowners near a steel plant could pursue a nuisance claim for noise that reduced their property values, even without physical damage.

Data center noise cases are coming. The legal theory is sound. What has been missing is plaintiffs willing to file.

Precedent	A court decision that future courts are expected to follow in similar cases. The first big ruling on data center noise will shape every case that comes after it.

6.2 VIBRATION

Several Loudoun County residents have reported physical vibrations—the effects described at the start of this chapter. In Aurora, Illinois, the proposed data center ordinance included vibration monitoring as a condition of approval.

Document vibration the same way you document noise (see the "Document Everything" section at the end of this chapter). Place a glass of water on a flat surface and photograph it—visible ripples are evidence.

If vibration damages your property, such as cracked foundations or shifted walls, the claim moves from nuisance to property damage. The developer is liable for the cost of repair.

6.3 LIGHT

Data centers operate around the clock. That means security lighting, parking lot lights, and perimeter lights burn all night.

Light that spills from one property onto another is called light trespass. Courts in most states recognize it as a form of nuisance.

The nuisance claim works the same way as for noise.

6.3.1 *What to Do About It*

Check whether your local code has a light trespass ordinance. Some cities require outdoor lights to use full cutoff fixtures that point downward, not outward. If the data center's lights violate the ordinance, file a code enforcement complaint.

If code enforcement does not solve the problem, the nuisance claim is available.

Document the light. Take photographs at night from your property. A light meter costs about $30 and can measure the intensity in lux. That measurement becomes evidence.

Tip

Organizations like DarkSky International publish guidelines for acceptable outdoor lighting levels. Their standards can support your case even if your local code does not address light trespass.

6.4 WATER

Water may be the most serious long-term impact of a data center on your property. A single large facility can consume up to 5 million gallons of water per day.

That water comes from somewhere—often the same aquifer or surface water supply that feeds your well or your town's water system.

6.4.1 Water Rights Vary by State

Water law varies by state. The three main systems:

- **Riparian rights (most eastern states).** You share water with other users along the same source. Overuse by one user can be grounds for a claim.
- **Prior appropriation (most western states).** Whoever claimed water first has priority—"first in time, first in right."
- **Permit-based systems.** Some states require permits for any large withdrawal. A data center that skipped the permit or got one without adequate review gives you a legal opening.

Ask a water rights attorney which system applies to you.

6.4.2 The Scale of the Problem

Google's Council Bluffs, Iowa, data center consumed more than 1 billion gallons of water in 2024—the most of any Google facility. In Mesa, Arizona, a hyperscale data center was contracted to consume up to 4 million gallons per day. In many communities, data centers pay lower bulk water rates than residents. That disparity is worth investigating with your local water authority.

If the data center pays less per gallon than you do, you are subsidizing its operations. Ask your local water authority whether any customer receives a bulk discount. Bring the answer to the next city council meeting.

6.4.3 When Wells Go Dry

In western Prince William County, Virginia, residents rely on private wells. When a large facility pumps from the same aquifer, it can create what hydrogeologists call a "cone of depression"—a dip in the water table around the pumping site. Wells within that cone may produce less water. Some may go dry entirely.

If your well goes dry or your water pressure drops after a data center starts operating, document the change. Record your water level before and after. Keep your well records—that documentation is the foundation of a legal claim.

Talk to your neighbors who also rely on wells. If multiple wells show declining levels, the pattern is stronger evidence than any single well. A hydrogeologist can map the cone of depression and connect it to the data center's pumping.

If you are on a municipal water system, ask your utility for its capacity report. If the data center's projected use exceeds surplus capacity, that is a problem the utility should address before construction begins.

In Caddo Parish, Louisiana, water use killed the deal. Three residents sued the City of Shreveport in January 2026 over a proposed data center. The project planned to pull 1.5 million gallons per day from Caddo Lake, with plans to increase to 5 million. It would also draw millions of gallons from Cross Lake, the city's drinking water source. Caddo Lake is home to threatened species, and no one even knew who would operate the facility. The planning commission voted it down 4–4 after documents showed 7.5 million gallons per day of total water use. But the city council overturned the denial 7–0. As of early 2026, the lawsuit is still pending.

If the data center discharges warm water into a stream or lake, see Chapter 5 for how to check for discharge permits and file comments.

6.5 PROPERTY VALUES

If a data center is built near your home, you may worry that your property is worth less. That worry is reasonable. But proving it in court is harder than you might expect.

6.5.1 *The Evidence Gap*

There is no large-scale, peer-reviewed study on how data centers affect nearby home prices. The evidence gap works in both directions.

A 2025 George Mason University study found that homes closer to data centers in Northern Virginia actually sold for more—because data centers cluster near strong roads, reliable power, and jobs. But Northern Virginia is the most mature data center market in the world. A facility surrounded by 174 others in a high-income area is different from a 500-acre campus next to a soybean farm in rural Indiana.

The absence of data does not mean the absence of harm. It means the harm has not been measured.

6.5.2 How Property Value Claims Work

The legal theory is called "diminution in value." You compare what your property was worth before the data center arrived to what it is worth after. The difference is your damages.

To prove this, you need appraisals. Get your property appraised now, before the data center is built or starts operating. A professional appraisal costs $300 to $500. If you live within a mile of a proposed data center, it is worth the investment—this baseline protects a future claim.

Save listings of comparable homes in your area. If values drop after the facility opens, a second appraisal shows the change. If you sell for less than the earlier appraisal, the gap is your loss—and your evidence.

The strongest property value claims are tied to a specific harm—noise, light, vibration, or water loss. A court is more likely to award damages when you can point to a data center running at 70 decibels on your property line. A vague claim that your house is worth less, without a specific cause, is harder to prove.

Ask your attorney about the statute of limitations. In many states, the clock starts running when the harm becomes apparent—not when you get around to filing. The deadline to sue may be shorter than you expect.

Most states require sellers to disclose known material facts that affect property value. A noise-producing industrial facility next door likely qualifies. If a buyer backs out or demands a lower price because of the data center, that transaction becomes evidence of diminished value.

6.5.3 The White County Model

White County, Indiana, adopted a condition that no other community has matched. When the county approved a data center after its moratorium, it required a 20-year property value guarantee. If a neighbor's property value drops because of the data center, the developer must make up the difference.

That provision was negotiated before the building went up. It is easier to get protections before approval than after. See Chapter 7 for how to negotiate these terms.

6.6 CONSTRUCTION IMPACTS

Before the data center operates, it gets built. Construction on a large data center campus lasts 12 to 24 months and generates serious impacts.

Truck traffic. A single data center can require thousands of concrete truck deliveries, heavy equipment hauls, and material shipments. Roads not designed for heavy loads develop potholes and cracks. Traffic backing up behind construction trucks delays school buses and commuters.

Dust and noise. Earth-moving, grading, and foundation work produce dust that settles on nearby homes and vehicles. Construction noise from pile-driving, excavation, and equipment operation can exceed 90 decibels at the site boundary.

Stormwater runoff. Clearing hundreds of acres of trees or farmland for a data center campus changes how water flows across the land. Without proper sediment controls, rain carries topsoil into streams and drainage ditches. If you notice increased flooding or muddy water in your creek after construction begins, report it to your state environmental agency.

Construction impacts are temporary, but they are not minor. If the developer did not submit a traffic management plan and a stormwater pollution prevention plan, ask why. Both should be conditions of approval.

6.6.1 How to Monitor Construction

If you live near the site, monitor construction yourself. Your records become evidence if you need to file a complaint or a claim later.

Dust. Photograph visible dust plumes from your property or a public road. Check the erosion controls at the site boundary—silt fencing that has fallen over or been buried by dirt is not working. Report missing or damaged controls to code enforcement and your state environmental agency.

Stormwater. After a rain, photograph turbid or discolored water in ditches, streams, or drainage channels near the site. Sediment-laden runoff may violate the site's stormwater permit. Report it to the state agency that issued the permit.

Truck traffic. Count trucks by time of day for at least one week. Photograph road damage: potholes, cracked shoulders, rutted edges. Include the date in each photo. Send the photos to your county roads department and the planning board.

Dewatering discharge. If the contractor pumps groundwater during excavation, note where the discharge goes and what it looks like. Clear water is normal. Cloudy or brown discharge may violate the contractor's permit.

6.7 Lawsuits That Are Happening Now

Data center lawsuits are no longer rare. Here are the cases that show how private law is being used.

6.7.1 Prince William Digital Gateway

In August 2025, a Virginia circuit court voided the rezoning for a 2,100-acre data center corridor near Manassas. The project, 23 million square feet across 37 buildings, would have been the largest data center campus in the world.

The plaintiffs were an HOA and 11 residents. They argued that the county's public notice did not comply with state law. The court agreed and struck down the rezoning.

QTS, Compass Datacenters, and the county appealed. As of late 2025, construction is barred while the appeal moves forward.

Eleven residents and a homeowners association stopped a $25 billion project. The tool was a procedural challenge—the public notice was defective. It shows what organized residents can do.

6.7.2 Saline Township, Michigan

In Saline Township, Michigan, a developer sued the township after the board denied rezoning for a large data center. The township, population 2,277, settled under pressure. The consent judgment allowed the data center to proceed in exchange for $4 million for an agricultural land preservation trust and $2 million for a community investment fund.

A resident living 256 yards from the planned site filed a motion to intervene. She alleged the township negotiated the settlement outside of public view, violating Michigan's Open Meetings Act.

Even after a settlement, residents may have standing to challenge it if the process was not transparent.

6.7.3 Montgomery County, Missouri

Residents formed Preserve Montgomery County LLC in late 2025 and sued the county in February 2026 over a proposed data center. Forming an LLC gives a group legal standing, limits individual liability, and lets the group hire an attorney as a single client.

These cases share patterns. Procedural challenges work—defective notice alone voided a \$25 billion project. Multiple plaintiffs are stronger than one. Organizations like the Southern Environmental Law Center and Earthjustice often provide free representation.

6.8 FINDING A LAWYER

If you have a legal claim, you need a lawyer.

6.8.1 What Kind of Lawyer

Match the lawyer to the claim:

- **Noise, light, or property value** — a nuisance or property damage attorney. Search "nuisance attorney" or "property rights attorney" plus your state.
- **Water contamination, air quality, or endangered species** — an environmental litigation attorney.
- **Zoning challenges** — a land use attorney.

Some cases involve all three. A good lawyer will tell you if you need someone with different experience.

6.8.2 What It Costs

Land use and environmental attorneys charge several hundred dollars per hour. A contested zoning case can run into the tens of thousands of dollars; environmental litigation can cost even more because of expert witnesses and discovery. Rates vary widely by market and case complexity—get multiple quotes.

> **Discovery** The part of a lawsuit where both sides must share their documents, records, and evidence with each other before trial. It is expensive and time-consuming, but it also forces the other side to reveal what it knows.

Those numbers are real. But there are ways to reduce the burden.

Contingency fees. Some firms take nuisance and property damage cases on contingency. You pay nothing up front. The firm takes a percentage of the judgment or settlement—typically 33 to 40%. If the firm loses, you owe nothing.

Contingency is more common for cases with clear, measurable damages: a well that went dry, a property value that dropped, medical bills from noise-related health problems.

Pro bono organizations. Several national organizations provide free legal help to communities fighting environmental harms.

The Southern Environmental Law Center is already active in data center cases, representing the Colleton County plaintiffs and leading the legal threat against xAI.

Earthjustice litigates environmental cases at no cost to clients through 15 offices and a community partnerships program.

The Environmental Law Institute's Pro Bono Clearinghouse connects communities with volunteer attorneys. Fair Shake Environmental Legal Services provides pro bono and sliding-scale help to individuals and grassroots groups. The Institute for Justice fights property rights and eminent domain cases at no cost to property owners.

Law school clinics. Many law schools have environmental law clinics that take real cases—Emory's Turner Clinic and Stanford's Environmental Law Clinic are two examples. The work is free and supervised by experienced professors.

6.8.3 *When to Contact a Lawyer*

The best time is before the hearing, not after the approval. A lawyer can review the permit application, identify weaknesses, and help you prepare testimony that builds a record for a future challenge.

If you wait until after approval, the appeal window is usually 30 days. A lawyer who reviews the case months later has less to work with.

Many attorneys offer a free initial consultation. Use that call to ask: is there a claim here? What should I be documenting? What deadlines am I facing?

6.8.4 Group Actions

You do not have to sue alone. Most data center lawsuits involve multiple plaintiffs—11 residents in the Prince William case, 3 in Caddo Parish. Sharing the cost makes litigation affordable and sends a stronger signal to the court.

Splitting costs across ten or twenty households makes a retainer affordable and creates the kind of case an attorney will take on contingency.

In some cases, a local government can file a public nuisance action on behalf of the entire community. The California Supreme Court has ruled that public entities may hire private attorneys on contingency to prosecute public nuisance claims.

Legal challenges work. Lawsuits, moratoria, denied permits, and withdrawn applications have stopped or slowed projects across the country.

6.8.5 If the Data Center Is Already Operating

If the data center is already built and running, your options are still real. Document current conditions now: noise, water, property values. The statute of limitations for nuisance claims varies by state—typically two to three years from when the harm becomes apparent, though some states allow up to six. Contact an attorney promptly. Chapter 7 and Chapter 9 cover negotiation and organizing tools that work after construction.

6.9 DOCUMENT EVERYTHING

The strength of your case depends on your evidence. Start collecting it now—before you hire a lawyer, before the data center opens.

6.9.1 The Basics: Every Entry

Every observation needs five things: who observed it, what happened, when (date and time), where (exact location), and the weather conditions.

Use a dedicated notebook or app. Write in ink. If you make a mistake, cross it out with a single line and initial it—never erase or white out. Timestamp every entry.

Photograph and video record what you see. Turn on geotagging so your phone embeds the location in the file.

Back up digital files the same day—to a cloud folder, a USB drive, or both. A phone that gets lost or broken takes your evidence with it.

6.9.2 Chain of Custody

Chain of custody is the record showing who collected evidence, who handled it, and how it was stored. Without it, a water sample or noise recording can be challenged as contaminated or altered.

Label every sample: your name, the date, the time, and how you collected it. Photograph the labeled sample before sending it to the lab. Keep original digital files unedited—work on copies if you want to crop or annotate. Log who handled each piece of evidence and when.

6.9.3 Well Water

If you rely on a private well, test it before construction begins. That baseline is the most important evidence you will collect.

Ask the lab to test for coliform bacteria, nitrates, hardness, conductivity, turbidity, heavy metals, and volatile organic compounds (VOCs). Also request tests for any contaminants named in the developer's permits.

Find a certified lab through your state environmental agency's website or the EPA's drinking water lab locator at https://www.epa.gov/dwlabcert. The lab provides collection bottles and instructions. Follow the instructions exactly—a sample collected wrong is a sample thrown away. A standard panel costs $50 to $150.

Test quarterly during construction and after the facility opens. Record your well's static water level (before pumping) and dynamic level (after five minutes of pumping), plus the flow rate. Keep all original lab reports. If your neighbors also have wells, test on the same schedule so results can be compared.

6.9.4 Noise

Not all decibel readings are equal. Most noise ordinances use dBA, which filters out low frequencies. Data center hum is low-frequency—it may read much louder on the dBC scale, which treats all frequencies equally. Record both if your meter supports it.

Measure systematically: multiple readings per session, note wind conditions, and use a calibrated meter if you plan to use the data in court. See Appendix B for the full measurement protocol.

A single reading is not evidence. A 30-day log showing the noise ordinance was exceeded on 23 of 30 nights is evidence. The pattern is what matters.

Smartphone apps like the NIOSH Sound Level Meter are useful for screening, but they are not court-grade instruments. For litigation, you will need readings from a calibrated meter or a professional acoustical engineer.

6.9.5 Air Quality

PurpleAir sensors start at about \$240, measure fine particulate pollution (PM2.5) around the clock, and upload data to a public map. A sensor on your property creates a permanent record of air quality before and after the data center operates.

For regulatory monitoring data, check the EPA's AirNow website at https://www.airnow.gov.

Log every diesel generator event you observe: start time, stop time, duration, and whether you see visible smoke or smell exhaust. Generator testing and outage events produce the heaviest emissions.

For formal monitoring beyond what you can do yourself, contact your state environmental agency. Some agencies lend portable air monitors to communities near industrial facilities. Connect any air quality claims to the facility's emission permits (see Chapter 5).

6.9.6 Light

Photograph from the same spot each time, using the same camera settings if possible. Use a tripod to keep the framing consistent. A lux meter (about \$30) measures light intensity at your property line.

One bright night does not make a case. Multiple consecutive nights with readings above your baseline do. A week of dated photos and lux readings establishes a pattern that supports a nuisance claim.

6.9.7 *Property Value and Health*

For appraisal guidance, see the property value section earlier in this chapter.

If you experience sleep loss, headaches, or anxiety after the data center begins operating, see your doctor. Ask for a written record that links your symptoms to the noise or other exposure. Medical records that document a timeline support a damages claim.

☑ What You Can Do

Property rights action plan:

1. **Start an observation log.** Record baseline noise, light, water levels, and property value before the data center opens. See Appendix B for observation log templates. Dated entries with chain of custody are the foundation of any legal claim.

2. **Check your local noise ordinance.** If the data center exceeds the decibel limit at your property line, file a code enforcement complaint. This creates an official record even if the fine is small.

3. **Know your water rights.** Determine whether your state follows riparian, prior appropriation, or permit-based rules. If you have a private well, monitor your water level and flow rate. A drop after the data center opens is evidence.

4. **Talk to your neighbors.** Lawsuits are stronger and cheaper when multiple households file together. Start the conversation early.

5. **Find a lawyer.** Contact a nuisance, environmental, or land use attorney. Ask about contingency fees. Check whether the Southern Environmental Law Center, Earthjustice, or the Environmental Law Institute's Pro Bono Clearinghouse can help.

CHAPTER SEVEN

Fight at the Table

Henrico County, Virginia, created a $60 million affordable housing trust fund. The money comes from data center tax revenue—and only from data center tax revenue. In its first 17 months, the fund helped finance 119 homes for families earning 60 to 120% of the area median income.

The fund exists because the county negotiated.

Not every fight is about stopping a project. Some communities have decided the project is coming and shifted to a different question: what does the community get in return?

What follows is about that question. It covers community benefit agreements, tax abatement terms, clawback provisions, decommissioning bonds, and the conditions that make a deal worth accepting or rejecting.

The key principle: negotiate from a position of strength, not desperation. The developer wants your land, your water, your electricity, and your approval. Those are valuable. Do not give them away for a press release and a ribbon cutting.

Every term in the agreement should answer the central question from Chapter 2: *if the optimistic projection turns out to be wrong, who bears the downside risk?* If the jobs do not appear, who keeps the tax break? If the water runs short, who gets cut first? A good deal puts the risk on the party that made the projection.

7.1 COMMUNITY BENEFIT AGREEMENTS

A community benefit agreement is a contract between a developer and the community. The developer commits to specific benefits in exchange for community support or approval: money, jobs, environmental protections.

CBAs are still uncommon in data center deals. But they are growing. Brookings has called them "necessary for data centers."

The key to a CBA is that it is legally binding. A developer's promise at a public hearing is not a contract. A press release is not a contract. A CBA is a contract, enforceable in court, with specific terms and consequences for violation.

Have your own attorney review any CBA before you sign it. The developer has a legal team that drafted the agreement to protect their interests. You need someone who reads it to protect yours. Make sure the agreement is recorded so it binds future owners—if the data center is sold, you want the new owner on the hook for the same terms.

7.1.1 Getting a CBA Started

Who proposes a CBA? Anyone can. Ask your county board to form a community negotiating committee as a condition of the permit. If the board will not act, a neighborhood group can approach the developer directly. The developer wants community support—give them a way to earn it.

If the developer says "take it or leave it," your bargaining power comes from the permit process. A conditional use permit gives the planning board authority to attach conditions whether the developer agrees or not (see Chapter 3). If the project is by-right, your options shift to litigation (Chapter 6) and organizing (Chapter 9).

> **⚠ Caution**
>
> If you cannot afford an attorney yet, watch for these red flags in any proposed agreement:
>
> 1. Vague language like "up to" or "reasonable efforts" instead of specific numbers.
> 2. No enforcement mechanism—who checks compliance, and what happens if they violate the terms?
> 3. Clauses that let the developer modify terms or assign the agreement to a new owner without community approval.

7.1.2 Strong Terms vs. Weak Terms

No deal is all good or all bad. A single agreement can have a strong employment clause and a weak water provision. What matters is whether each term is specific, measurable, and enforceable—and whether the community gave up more than it got back.

Here is what to look for, clause by clause.

Employment floors. Cedar Rapids, Iowa, set the standard. Google must maintain at least 31 full-time jobs paying $26.20 or more per hour; QTS must maintain at least 15 jobs per phase. Those are binding minimums with specific numbers, not "up to 200 jobs" or "competitive salaries." Compare Sidney, Ohio: Amazon received a 30-year, 100% abatement worth $180 to $350 million for 75 jobs—$2.4 to $4.7 million per job—with no stated wage floor.

Water and environmental caps. Lancaster, Pennsylvania, capped CoreWeave's water use at 20,000 gallons per day—a hard daily limit, not an annual average that can hide peak-demand spikes. El Paso required Meta to use closed-loop cooling and file annual sustainability reports on water and electricity use. Both are measurable. Compare Wilmington, Ohio, where Amazon's $4 billion campus received a 30-year property tax abatement with a 30% PILOT offset—effectively 70%. The agreement contains no provisions for water, noise, or air quality.

Revenue dedication. Henrico County, Virginia, did not negotiate a traditional CBA. Instead, the county directed data center tax revenue into the housing trust fund described at the start of this chapter—$60 million and counting. The strength: the funding stream is automatic and does not depend on annual political decisions.

Direct payments vs. one-time windfalls. Cedar Rapids gets $400,000 a year from Google and up to $18 million over 20 years from QTS—recurring cash that the community can plan around. Wilmington got a single payment of $1.85 million for a $4 billion project—then nothing, for 30 years.

Transparency. Any agreement involving public money should be public. The Ohio deal's terms were hidden for 18 months under an NDA. Genesee County, New York, approved $801 million in tax breaks for Stream Data Centers for 125 jobs—$6.4 million per job. The scale of that subsidy only became clear after investigative reporting, not public disclosure.

The per-job test. Divide the total tax break by the number of permanent jobs.

Subsidy	Money or tax breaks that the government gives to a company to attract it to an area. The cost is covered by other taxpayers—through higher taxes or fewer services.

Traditional manufacturing subsidies run about $100,000 per job; $200,000 is expensive. Sidney's deal costs $2.4 to $4.7 million per job. Genesee County's costs $6.4 million per job. If a board member cannot defend that number at a public hearing, the terms are too generous.

Remember: "up to 200 jobs" can mean 10 jobs. If it is not a binding minimum in the agreement, it is not a commitment.

7.1.3 Timing Matters

A deal negotiated before approval gives the community maximum bargaining power. After construction, the developer holds the cards.

In Memphis, Tennessee, the city council directed 25% of xAI's property tax revenue—up to $100 million—into public benefit projects within five miles of the facility. But the facility sits in Boxtown, a low-income neighborhood that has been underserved for decades. Residents worry the money will flow elsewhere. Get your terms before the first shovel hits the ground.

7.1.4 *What to Push For*

What your community can get depends on its bargaining position—how much the developer needs your site, your water, your grid capacity, or your approval. A township of 5,000 people with one viable site has different bargaining power than a county with a dozen competing proposals. But every community can push for more than the developer's opening offer.

Real communities have won every one of the terms below. Not every term will be available in every negotiation, but each one establishes a floor you can point to.

Recurring payments, not one-time gifts. Annual cash payments give the community a funding stream it can plan around. One-time payments—like the $1.85 million for a $4 billion project in the Ohio example above—are easy for the developer and cheap relative to the deal.

Binding job and wage minimums. A contract that says "at least 50 full-time employees at $25 per hour or above" means something. "Up to 200 jobs at competitive salaries" does not.

Hard caps on water and noise. Daily limits, not annual averages. Consequences for violations, not just reporting requirements.

No NDAs on public terms. The developer's proprietary technology may be confidential, but the terms of a public benefit agreement are the public's business.

Annual public reporting. El Paso requires annual sustainability reports from Meta on water and electricity use. If the developer will not report on what it promised, the promise is worth less than the paper it is printed on.

A decommissioning plan. What happens when the facility closes? See Section 7.5 for details.

Specific environmental protections. Closed-loop cooling. EPA Tier 4 emission standards for backup generators. Waste management plans. The more specific the terms, the harder they are to ignore.

7.2 THE NDA PROBLEM

Nondisclosure agreements are the single biggest obstacle to fair data center deals.

Developers routinely ask local officials to sign NDAs before sharing project details. The NDA prevents officials from telling residents what the project is, who is building it, what it will use, and what the community is giving up.

In Bessemer, Alabama, city officials signed NDAs with the developer. Residents could not learn basic facts about the deal. In one Ohio deal, the terms of a $4 billion project were kept secret for 18 months. In Tucson, Arizona, and Indianapolis, Indiana, projects failed after the public discovered that officials had signed NDAs.

The rule should be simple: any agreement involving public money, public land, public water, or public infrastructure is a public document. If the developer insists on an NDA as a precondition for talks, that tells you something about the deal.

Good Jobs First recommends that state legislatures prohibit data center developers from imposing NDAs on state or local public officials. If your state does not have this protection, push your lawmakers to add it.

7.3 Tax Abatements

Chapter 2 covered the scale of data center tax breaks. Here is what to do about them when you are at the negotiating table.

7.3.1 The Spiral

Virginia's data center tax break started at $1.5 million a year. By 2025, it cost $1.6 billion—more than a thousand times the original estimate. Data centers accounted for 53% of all Virginia incentive spending between 2015 and 2024. That is what happens when a tax break has no cap, no sunset, and no review. For the full legislative history, see Chapter 4.

7.3.2 The Cost-Per-Job Problem

Data center tax breaks are expensive per job because data centers employ very few people. Genesee County: $6.4 million per job. One Ohio deal: $2.4 to $4.7 million per job. Lockport, New York: $2.4 million per job.

A manufacturing plant that receives $100,000 per job in subsidies is considered expensive. Data center subsidies run 20 to 60 times higher.

When the developer presents a jobs number, apply the per-job test from above: divide the total tax break by permanent jobs. Then ask the board: can we justify that number to our residents?

7.3.3 The Disclosure Problem

At least 36 states have data center subsidy programs. Twelve do not report even the total amount of revenue they lose.

Texas reports which companies receive breaks but nothing else—no subsidy amounts, no job creation numbers, not even project locations. Virginia does not disclose which companies benefit from its $1.6 billion annual exemption.

If your state will not tell you what the breaks cost, you cannot evaluate whether they are working. Push your state lawmakers to require full disclosure of every data center incentive deal, including the company name, subsidy amount, job commitments, and actual performance.

7.3.4 Structuring a Better Abatement

Tax breaks are not always bad. A short-term abatement with strong terms and real accountability can be a reasonable trade. A 30-year, 100% abatement with no conditions is a giveaway. If your community is considering an abatement, push for these safeguards.

A sunset clause.

Sunset clause	An expiration date built into a law or agreement. Without one, a tax break can last decades longer than anyone intended.

No tax break should last 50 years. Set a term—10 or 15 years is reasonable—and build in a review before renewal. Indiana offers up to 50 years for investments over $750 million. That is a commitment that outlasts the building.

A performance trigger. The tax break should shrink if the developer does not meet its promises. The Ohio abatement described above gave the developer a 30-year break for 75 jobs. The agreement should have tied the abatement percentage to actual job creation: full abatement for 75 or more jobs, reduced for fewer.

A payment in lieu of taxes (PILOT).

> **PILOT** — Payment In Lieu Of Taxes—a fixed annual payment a company makes instead of regular property taxes. Usually much lower than the full tax bill, but it ensures schools and services get something rather than nothing.

Even with an abatement, the developer should make annual payments to the community. A PILOT ensures that schools, fire departments, and roads receive funding even when the property tax is waived. That deal's PILOT is $50 million over 15 years, with 50% going to schools. That is better than nothing. But $50 million is a small fraction of a $180 to $350 million abatement.

A local opt-out. Indiana is considering legislation that would require data centers to pay local governments 1% of the sales taxes waived by the state through a PILOT structure. The 1% figure is a modest step. Push for 3–5% of gross revenue, with annual escalation tied to CPI. But even at 1%, it establishes the principle that local communities should receive compensation for state tax breaks granted within their borders.

Push your state lawmakers to allow local governments to opt out of state-level data center incentives. If the state wants to give tax breaks, the state should pay for them—not the local school district.

An independent cost-benefit analysis. Before approving any tax break, require an independent analysis of whether the community comes out ahead. The analysis should compare the cost of the abatement to the actual revenue the project will generate over its lifetime. It should account for infrastructure costs such as roads, water, sewer, and grid upgrades, not just tax payments.

Most economic impact studies are commissioned by the developer. Commission your own.

In February 2026, Illinois Governor JB Pritzker proposed a two-year freeze on data center tax incentives—the first such proposal by a sitting governor (see Chapter 4).

7.4 CLAWBACKS

A clawback is a provision that lets the community take back tax breaks if the developer does not deliver what it promised. In theory, clawbacks protect the public. In practice, most are too weak to matter.

7.4.1 Why Most Clawbacks Fail

About 75% of incentive programs contain some form of penalty. But 84 of 178 programs studied by Good Jobs First have penalties weakened by discretion or exceptions. Officials often take a "good faith" approach and let companies off the hook.

The Ohio deal described above has a clawback provision. If the developer fails to comply with the agreement, the city can terminate the tax break and claw back three years of benefits. But the agreement also says that job estimates do not limit the abatement. If the jobs never appear, the clawback may never trigger.

7.4.2 What a Strong Clawback Looks Like

Good Jobs First recommends that clawbacks be automatic, not discretionary, and triggered by measurable benchmarks: job numbers, wage levels, investment thresholds. Their model formula includes a 20-year operating commitment, 5% per year reduction for unmet targets, and prevailing wage requirements (see Appendix B).

Every clawback should be in a written agreement posted on a public website. The agreement should identify the beneficial owner of the project—not the shell company on the permit. Applications for incentives should be posted online 90 days before any approval vote.

> **👍 What This Means for You**
>
> If the clawback depends on a vote of the same officials who gave away the money, it will not be used. Make it automatic. Tie it to numbers—job counts, wage levels, investment thresholds—that anyone can verify.

7.5 DECOMMISSIONING

What happens to a one-million-square-foot building when the technology moves on?

7.5.1   *The 20-Year Problem*

QTS, one of the largest data center operators, told Linn County, Iowa, supervisors that data center buildings may have a 20-year feasible lifespan. After 20 years, the building may be obsolete. The servers are gone. The cooling equipment is outdated. What remains is a concrete box the size of a small town.

Almost no community requires a decommissioning plan for data centers. By contrast, solar farms and wind turbines routinely require decommissioning bonds—money set aside to pay for removal when the project ends.

7.5.2   *What to Require*

Push for a decommissioning bond as a condition of approval. The bond should cover the cost of removing the building and restoring the site. It should be funded before construction begins.

Aurora, Illinois, proposed that decommissioning must include removal of obsolete equipment. Coweta County, Georgia, debated a decommissioning requirement during its 2025 data center ordinance. Residents asked for it. The final ordinance did not include it.

Surety bonds already exist for data center construction guarantees—extending them to decommissioning is straightforward. The question is whether communities will demand it.

7.5.3   *How to Size the Bond*

The bond should cover three things: removal of all equipment, demolition of the building, and restoration of the site to its prior condition.

Get an independent estimate from a demolition contractor, not from the developer. A one-million-square-foot industrial building may cost $10 million or more to demolish. Site restoration adds to the total: regrading, replanting, and soil remediation.

The surety should be independent—held by a bonding company, not by the developer. If the developer goes bankrupt in year 15, the bond ensures the community is not left with a concrete shell and a cleanup bill.

Review the bond amount every five years. Demolition costs rise with inflation. A bond sized in 2026 may be inadequate in 2040. Build an escalation clause into the agreement so the bond grows with the cost of removal.

Tip

If your county requires decommissioning bonds for solar farms or wind turbines, use that precedent. Ask your planning board: if we require a bond for a 50-acre solar farm, why not for a 100-acre data center? The analogy is direct and hard to argue against.

7.6 CONDITIONS OF APPROVAL

The "What to Push For" list above covers what goes in a CBA—a private contract. The conditions below go in the permit itself. The legal difference matters: permit conditions are enforceable by the government, even if the developer changes hands. A CBA binds only the parties who signed it. Put your strongest protections in both places.

Chapter 3 covered the basics of conditional use permits. What follows gives you specific numbers to bring to the hearing.

7.6.1 *Noise, Vibration, and Setbacks*

Noise. Albemarle County, Virginia, proposed limits of 60 decibels during the day, 55 at night. Aurora, Illinois, proposed 59/49 with 24-hour monitoring. Chandler, Arizona, requires zero net increase from the pre-construction baseline—the strongest standard. Ask for pre-construction measurements and post-construction monitoring by a licensed engineer.

Vibration. Data centers produce vibration from cooling equipment, generators, and transformers. In Prince William County, a resident reported that his headboard vibrated from a nearby facility. Aurora requires vibration monitoring at property lines. Include vibration standards alongside noise limits.

Setbacks. Fairfax County, Virginia: 200 feet from homes, 300 for generators. Linn County, Iowa: 1,000 feet from any home. Aurora: 1,500 feet between rooftop chillers and the nearest house.

Tie each setback to a specific harm. A 1,000-foot setback protects against noise. A 300-foot setback from generators protects against diesel exhaust. The more precise the justification, the harder it is to argue against.

7.6.2 Water, Generators, and Energy

Water. Albemarle County requires closed-loop cooling and bans groundwater use. Aurora banned evaporative cooling entirely. At least eight states have introduced water reporting bills; governors in California, New Jersey, and Virginia vetoed them.

Generators. Chandler limits testing to weekday business hours. Albemarle requires EPA Tier 4 emission standards. Aurora bans rooftop generators entirely. Ask how many hours per year the generators will run and whether combined emissions trigger a Clean Air Act permit (see Chapter 5).

Energy efficiency. Aurora requires a Power Use Effectiveness (PUE) of 1.2—meaning no more than 20% of electricity lost to cooling and overhead. It also requires on-site renewable energy at 25% of peak demand, or battery storage for 15 minutes at 50% capacity.

7.6.3 Screening and Geographic Restrictions

Screening. Fairfax County requires all equipment enclosed or screened, plus facade variations every 150 feet. If the data center is near homes, insist on landscaping buffers, architectural standards, and light shielding.

Geographic exclusions. Atlanta banned data centers within its 22-mile Beltline overlay district after demand consumed 730 megawatts. Your zoning code can exclude data centers from specific areas—residential zones, historic districts, watersheds, or areas near schools and transit. If the code says "no data centers within one mile of a school," the developer cannot negotiate around it. That is the power of zoning.

7.6.4 A Model Checklist

Here is a summary of conditions that leading communities have adopted. Bring this list to your next planning hearing.

1. Noise: 55 dBA or lower at the property line at night, with 24-hour monitoring.

2. Setbacks: 1,000 feet from the nearest home. 300 feet for generators and heavy equipment.

3. Water: closed-loop cooling required. No groundwater withdrawals. Daily use cap in the agreement.

4. Generators: testing limited to weekday business hours. EPA Tier 4 emission standards. No rooftop generators.

5. Energy: PUE standard of 1.2 or better. Renewable energy or battery storage requirement.

6. Screening: all equipment enclosed or screened. Facade variations required. Full cutoff lighting.

7. Vibration: monitoring at property lines. Maximum levels established and maintained.

8. Reporting: annual public reports on water, energy, noise, jobs, and emissions.

9. Decommissioning: surety bond for building removal and site restoration.

10. Independent monitoring: pre-construction baselines and post-construction studies by engineers chosen by the community.

No single community has adopted all of these conditions. But every one of them has been adopted somewhere. Print this list and bring it to the next hearing. Where the developer's terms fall short, ask why—on the record.

7.7 YOUR BIGGEST ADVANTAGE: TIME

Developers face intense pressure to build fast. Hyperscalers demand capacity on tight schedules. If the developer misses the window, the tenant may choose a different site.

The developer needs your approval on a schedule. Delay costs them money. That gives you bargaining power.

A moratorium buys six to twelve months of study time. A conditional use permit process adds weeks or months of review. A public records request that reveals secret meetings slows momentum. Communities that used moratoria as negotiating tools—not just delays—got better deals (see Chapter 3 for examples).

Do not let the developer set the timeline. If the developer says "we need a decision by next month," that is their problem, not yours. Rushing benefits only one side.

7.7.1 Hire Your Own Experts

Do not rely on the developer's studies. The developer's noise study will show compliance. The developer's economic impact study will show job creation. These studies may be accurate, or they may be designed to reach a favorable conclusion.

Push your planning board to hire independent consultants—paid by the developer but chosen by the community. Many conditional use permits require the applicant to fund the community's review. The cost of an independent noise study is trivial compared to the tax breaks the developer is requesting. If the developer refuses to fund an independent review, note that refusal on the record.

To find consultants, search for "environmental noise consulting" or "fiscal impact analysis" firms in your region. Your state's municipal league can provide referrals. The National League of Cities, PennFuture, and the American Association for the Advancement of Science have all published free resources to help communities evaluate data center proposals.

7.7.2 Common Developer Arguments

You will hear some of these at the hearing. Some are bluffs. Some contain a grain of truth. Knowing the difference matters.

"These conditions will kill the project." Maybe. But communities across the country have adopted noise limits, water caps, and setback requirements, and projects were still built. Ask the developer to identify specifically which condition is unworkable, and why. If the answer is vague, the objection is a negotiating tactic.

"No other community requires this." Aurora, Albemarle, Fairfax, and Chandler all adopted strong conditions. Bring their ordinances to the hearing.

"The market will solve this." The market built data centers by right with no noise limits, no water caps, and 50-year tax breaks. Conditions exist because the market did not solve it.

106

"We will take the project somewhere else." Sometimes this is a bluff. Sometimes it is true—developers do have other sites. But a developer willing to accept reasonable conditions elsewhere and not in your community is telling you something about how it plans to operate.

"The tax break is standard." Ask them to name three comparable deals with the same per-job cost. Ohio's data center breaks cost $2.4 to $6.4 million per job—20 to 60 times more than other industries. "Standard" is not the same as "justified."

Michigan set the national standard for ratepayer protections: 19-year contracts, 80% minimum billing, and data center load shed before residential customers (see Chapter 4 for the full case study). Every community should ask for the same.

☑ What You Can Do

Negotiation action plan:

1. **Demand a community benefit agreement.** The agreement should include direct payments, job minimums with wages, water and noise caps, and annual public reporting. Reject NDAs on the agreement itself.

2. **Limit tax abatements.** Push for a 10-to-15-year sunset, performance triggers tied to actual job creation, and a PILOT that funds schools and services even during the abatement period.

3. **Require strong clawbacks.** The clawback should be mandatory, not at the discretion of officials. It should reduce benefits by 5% for each year job targets are missed. The agreement should be posted publicly.

4. **Require a decommissioning bond.** If your community requires bonds for solar or wind, demand one for data centers. The bond should cover building removal and site restoration.

5. **Set specific conditions.** Noise limits at the property line (55 dB or lower at night). Setbacks of at least 300 feet from homes. Closed-loop cooling. Generator testing limited to daytime hours. Pre- and post-construction monitoring by a licensed engineer.

CHAPTER EIGHT

Fight in the Boardroom

Amazon Employees for Climate Justice surveyed 800 of their coworkers in 2024. Only 14% said climate impacts are a key factor when Amazon leaders make business decisions. Fewer than 15% said the company tells the truth about its greenhouse gas emissions.

These are Amazon's own employees. They know what the company says in public. They also know what happens inside.

When government tools are not enough and lawsuits are too slow, the market offers another set of tools. Shareholders can file proposals. Employees can organize. Customers can demand changes.

Communities can pressure the companies that profit from data centers. Challenge them where they are most sensitive: in front of their investors, in their sustainability reports, and in the court of public opinion.

Here is how. You do not need wealth or stock. You need to know where to push.

8.1 SHAREHOLDER PROPOSALS

If you own stock in any company building data centers—Amazon, Microsoft, Google, Meta, Oracle, or others—you are a shareholder. That gives you the right to attend the annual meeting and vote on proposals. Even one share counts.

More important, institutional investors who own millions of shares are starting to ask hard questions about data center growth.

8.1.1   What Is Happening

Every year, shareholders file climate proposals at Amazon, Meta, Microsoft, and Alphabet. Most fail. But proposals that get 20% to 30% of the vote signal real investor concern—and generate press coverage you can use at local hearings.

The gap between these companies' climate promises and their actual emissions keeps growing. Alphabet's emissions rose nearly 50% since 2019. Meta's location-based emissions more than doubled. Cite these numbers in your next public comment—they come from the companies' own filings. That gap is what shareholder proposals are designed to expose.

8.1.2   Do Shareholder Proposals Work?

Most shareholder proposals fail. Average support for climate proposals dropped to 12.7% in 2025. Companies recommend a "no" vote, and most institutional investors follow the board's advice.

But proposals do not have to pass to matter. A proposal that gets 20% of the vote puts the issue on the record and generates press coverage. Some proposals lead to real change—after the 8,700-signature employee petition, Amazon published its first detailed emissions breakdown.

Climate proposals fell from 126 in 2024 to 80 in 2025, partly because of political pressure and changing SEC rules. But the proposals that do get filed are more focused than ever on data center growth.

8.1.3   How You Can Help

Owning stock is not required to influence a shareholder vote. What you need is allies who do.

Public pension funds are among the largest investors in Big Tech. Your state retirement system likely holds shares in all the major data center builders. Write to your state treasurer or pension fund board. Ask how they vote on climate and environmental proposals at Big Tech companies.

Check pending proposals before the next annual meeting. Go to the company's investor relations page and look for the proxy statement, usually filed 30 to 60 days before the meeting. You can also search the SEC's EDGAR database for the company name and "DEF 14A"—that is the proxy statement filing code. Proposals are listed inside.

Search for "[your state] pension fund proxy voting record" or check your state comptroller's website. Most public pension funds publish their votes by company and proposal. Find the climate or environmental proposal for whichever company is building in your community. If your fund voted "against," write the fund's investment committee and ask why—and send a copy to your state treasurer.

A letter from a voter to a pension fund trustee carries weight. A letter from 50 voters changes the conversation.

You do not need the fund to divest from Big Tech. You need it to vote "yes" on the next climate proposal. A single large fund switching its vote can push a proposal from 10% to 20% support—enough to put the board on notice. A one-page letter to your pension fund's investment committee can start the conversation. State which company you are concerned about, name the specific proposal, and ask how the fund plans to vote.

8.1.4 *Institutional Investors*

The largest investment firms—BlackRock, Vanguard, State Street—have pulled back from climate voting under political pressure. That makes your state pension fund's vote even more important.

Institutional investors still care about risk. They measure it using ESG (Environmental, Social, and Governance) ratings, which score companies on climate, workers' rights, and honest management. A company that faces water shortages, grid constraints, or regulatory crackdowns at its data center sites has material business risk. Frame your concerns in those terms—not just ethics, but money.

CalPERS, the New York State Common Retirement Fund, and CalSTRS are among the largest shareholders in Big Tech. If you live in one of those states, your retirement system has real influence.

Some pension funds are already taking action. The Ohio Carpenters' Pension Plan sued Oracle in January 2026 over concealed debt from its data center buildout. The full financial picture—and how to use it—is in the next section.

8.2   The Weak Balance Sheet

The developer's pitch makes data centers sound like a sure thing. The balance sheets tell a different story.

Oracle is the most indebted tech company in the world—more than $108 billion in total debt, with $248 billion in off-balance-sheet lease commitments tied mostly to data centers. In late 2025, its free cash flow turned negative by more than $10 billion in a single quarter. Shareholders filed a securities fraud class action in February 2026, alleging the company's AI spending was far outpacing revenue. Bondholders filed a separate suit, alleging Oracle hid plans for $38 billion in new debt when it sold $18 billion in bonds seven weeks earlier.

CoreWeave went public at $40 a share in March 2025. The stock hit $183. Then investors learned that nine-month-old construction delays at a key Texas facility had never been disclosed. The stock fell 34%. A class action followed.

Fermi Inc. went public in October 2025 at $21 a share, promising an 11-gigawatt nuclear-powered data center campus. Two months later, its anchor tenant walked away from a $150 million commitment. The stock fell 59%.

These are not isolated cases. As of early 2026, investors have filed securities lawsuits against more than 20 data center and AI infrastructure companies. Some of those companies—or companies like them—may be the ones proposing a project in your community.

8.2.1   *What This Means for Your Community*

A developer carrying $108 billion in debt may not be around to keep its 20-year promises. A company whose anchor tenant just walked away may not finish your project on time. Financial fragility shows up as missed construction deadlines, unfilled job commitments, and abandoned sites.

Use it in your negotiations. If the developer is publicly traded, search the SEC's EDGAR database for its most recent 10-K filing. Look for total debt, free cash flow, and risk factors mentioning construction delays or customer losses. Search for the company name plus "class action"—if investors are suing, the complaint describes the financial problems in plain English.

If your state pension fund has filed suit against the developer, that fund is a potential ally. Write to the fund's investment committee. Tell them a project from the same company is proposed in your community. Ask what the fund's position is.

Demand stronger financial protections in local deals: letters of credit, performance bonds, decommissioning guarantees. A company facing lawsuits from its own investors should have no objection to proving it can pay.

Private companies do not file 10-K reports. But their finances still surface through utility filings, bond prospectuses, and news coverage. Ask the planning board whether the developer has provided audited financial statements. If it has not, ask why.

8.3 Sustainability Reports: What They Say vs. What They Do

Every major tech company publishes an annual sustainability report. These reports describe the company's environmental goals, carbon emissions, water use, and renewable energy purchases. They are designed to make the company look good.

Read them anyway. They contain useful data—buried under pages of marketing language and carefully chosen metrics.

Start with the company's annual sustainability report and its most recent 10-K filing. Skip the executive summary. Go straight to the data tables.

Find the numbers for water consumption, electricity use, and greenhouse gas emissions. Then compare this year's numbers to last year's. The trend tells you what the marketing text will not.

8.3.1 The Gap Between Promises and Performance

Microsoft's electricity use nearly tripled between 2020 and 2024. Google's more than doubled. Both companies report declining carbon emissions, but only because they buy renewable energy certificates—paper credits that may not reduce actual emissions.

An analysis of Big Tech sustainability reports found what the authors called "obfuscation-by-complexity." The companies chose figures that tell the best story and used accounting methods that favor best-case results.

> **Greenwashing**   When a company makes itself look more environmentally friendly than it actually is—through misleading claims, selective data, or accounting tricks.

A study published in *npj Climate Action* found that 96% of companies with climate pledges exhibit at least one greenwashing risk indicator.

The most common tricks: reporting "market-based" emissions, which count purchased certificates as reductions, instead of "location-based" emissions, which measure what actually came out of the smokestack. Counting renewable energy credits bought in one state as offsetting coal power used in another. Reporting water "returned" to a different watershed than the one it was taken from.

Amazon claims to be 53% of the way to being "water positive." But that still means it consumes roughly twice as much water as it conserves.

Google consumed 6.4 billion gallons of water across its operations in 2023—and a single facility in Iowa used more than 1 billion gallons in 2024.

8.3.2   *How to Use This Information*

Pull numbers from sustainability reports and use them at public hearings.

If a data center is proposed in your community, cite the company's own water data. Tell the planning board: "This company's facilities used over 1 billion gallons of water at a single site last year. How much will this one use? They have not said."

If a Microsoft project is proposed, cite Microsoft's tripling of electricity use. Ask what that means for your power grid and your electric bill.

Companies spend millions producing these reports. Use them as evidence against the company's own claims. The numbers come from the companies' own filings. They are the most powerful evidence you have.

> **Tip**
>
> Sustainability reports are usually published in the spring. Download the PDF and search for "water," "electricity," and "emissions." The numbers you need are in the data tables, not in the marketing text. Save a copy—companies sometimes revise reports quietly after publication.

8.3.3 *How to Challenge the Numbers*

Across 594 tracked data center projects in the U.S., three out of four have no binding renewable energy commitment at all. Print that statistic and bring it to the planning commission. When a developer tells your planning board that its facility will use "100% renewable energy," ask three questions.

Is the renewable energy generated at the site, or purchased as certificates from a wind farm in another state? If certificates, the electricity powering the data center may still come from coal or gas.

Does the company report location-based emissions, meaning what actually came out of the smokestack, or market-based emissions, meaning what they paid someone else to generate? The difference can be enormous.

What is the trend? If the company reports declining emissions while electricity use is tripling, something does not add up.

ESG ratings from Sustainalytics, MSCI, and CDP can also serve as evidence. If Google's CDP score dropped because of water use, cite that in your testimony. If Amazon's Sustainalytics rating flagged climate risks, mention it in your letter to the pension fund. These are the numbers institutional investors use to make decisions.

8.4 THE LOBBYING MACHINE

The other side is not sitting still.

In 2025, the largest data center developers spent tens of millions of dollars on federal lobbying: Amazon, Microsoft, Google, Meta, Oracle, and others. The Data Center Coalition, an industry trade group, nearly tripled its lobbying budget in the third quarter of 2025.

The electronics manufacturing and equipment sector, which includes Microsoft and Oracle, spent more than $226 million on lobbying in 2025, in part to support data center growth. Ask your elected officials whether they have met with data center lobbyists—and whether those meetings are on the public calendar.

At the local level, the PR campaign is just as aggressive. Meta aired television ads in Washington, D.C., and eight state capitals featuring small-town imagery—farming equipment, diners, Main Street shops. A new AI trade group is organizing "data center field trips" for members of Congress and distributing talking points.

When you speak at a public hearing, the developer has a team of lobbyists, lawyers, and PR consultants behind them. That does not change the facts. But it explains why the developer's presentation looks so polished and why the local newspaper's coverage sometimes reads like a press release.

These tours show air-conditioned server rooms and gleaming lobbies. They do not show the diesel generators, the evaporative cooling towers, or the neighborhoods downwind.

When a reporter calls your group for comment, the developer's PR team has already placed their version of the story. Be ready. Have your own talking points prepared.

Lead with numbers from the company's own sustainability report. If the developer claims "100% renewable energy," respond with the distinction between certificates and actual power. If the developer claims minimal water use, cite the company's own data showing consumption rising 88% since 2019.

The industry also funds academic research that supports data center development. When a study appears showing data centers increase property values or create economic growth, check who paid for it. Industry-funded research is not automatically wrong. But it should be read with the same skepticism you would apply to any study paid for by the subject of the study.

When the developer cites a favorable study at the hearing, ask who funded it. If the answer is the developer or an industry trade group, say so on the record. The planning board should know.

> **⚠ Caution**
>
> Watch for "astroturf" campaigns—industry-funded groups that look like community organizations. If a new group appears in your area promoting data center benefits, check who funds it. Search the group name in lobbying databases at OpenSecrets.org. Virginia Connects spent at least $700,000 on digital marketing in Virginia in a single year—the website looked grassroots, but the funding was not.

8.5 PRESSURE THAT WORKS

Start with what is free and direct. If the company is publicly traded, look up shareholder proposals and write to your pension fund. If the facility is in a low-income area or near existing pollution sources, contact Earthjustice or the NAACP Environmental Justice program. If you know someone who works at the company, connect them with internal advocacy groups.

Employee organizing. A company can dismiss an outside critic. It cannot easily dismiss thousands of its own workers. Employees know what the sustainability report leaves out.

The open letter. In December 2025, the Sierra Club placed a full-page letter in the Indianapolis Star calling on Amazon, Google, Meta, and Microsoft to power their data centers with clean energy. Open letters generate press coverage, create a public record, and signal to investors that the issue is not going away.

Who gets stuck with the pollution. Data centers have concentrated in areas where land is cheap and zoning regulations are limited. They have also appeared in low-income neighborhoods already carrying heavy industrial pollution loads.

The xAI case in Mississippi (see Chapter 5) showed what happens when developers skip permits in overburdened communities. A citizen suit threat forced the company to remove unpermitted equipment.

In Louisiana, Meta's $10 billion data center will require three new methane gas plants in a region already burdened by petrochemical industry. In Memphis, xAI's Colossus facility sits in a neighborhood where the cancer risk is four times the national average.

If the data center in your community adds pollution to a place that already has more than its share, that strengthens your position in regulatory proceedings and court. EPA's EJScreen tool mapped pollution burdens by neighborhood before the agency removed it in 2025. A community mirror is available at screening-tools.com, and archived versions remain online. If your area scores at or above the 80th percentile for any pollution indicator, use it in hearings, filings, and the press.

Supply chain pressure. Your city government, school district, and hospital likely buy cloud services from Amazon, Google, or Microsoft. Ask the IT department: who is the provider?

A city council that buys cloud services can include sustainability reporting requirements in the next contract renewal. A school board can ask Google to disclose the environmental impact of the data centers serving the district. These are purchasing decisions, not hostile acts.

Marana, Arizona, took a different approach. After residents packed council chambers to oppose a data center, the town banned the water department from supplying potable water to data centers for cooling. The developer redesigned its facility around air cooling—a direct concession to the ordinance.

Enterprise customers are already moving in this direction—IT organizations have begun adding sustainability requirements into procurement requests. When a large employer in your community renews its cloud contract, that is a pressure point.

Consumer pressure. Individual consumer choices will not change these companies. But sharing data on energy and water use—at hearings, on social media, at the dinner table—creates the political conditions for regulation. Make the invisible visible.

Healthcare cost data. Researchers at UC Riverside and Caltech estimated that air pollution from U.S. data centers imposed $6.7 billion in public health costs in 2023 alone and could reach $12 to $21 billion a year by 2028. Diesel generators at data centers cause nearly 20,000 asthma symptom cases annually and impose $385 million in health burdens.

These numbers give the issue urgency beyond land use. When you can tell a county commissioner that the project will increase asthma cases in the district, the conversation changes. Health data is harder to dismiss than property value concerns.

Connect with local public health officials, hospital administrators, and school nurses who track respiratory illness rates. If they are willing to speak at a hearing, their testimony carries weight. A doctor who says "this project will increase asthma rates in our community" is harder to dismiss than a resident making the same claim.

Insurance and financial risk. Data centers face growing risks from water scarcity, grid instability, and climate change—the same problems they contribute to. If you are writing to a pension fund, frame the argument in terms of risk, not just ethics. A company that builds 20 data centers in water-stressed regions is making a business bet that investors should scrutinize.

You cannot outspend the tech industry. But shareholder proposals, pension fund letters, and sustainability report data cost almost nothing. Use market tools alongside government tools. A company facing a shareholder vote, a rate case challenge, and a zoning fight at the same time has to defend on every front.

☑ What You Can Do

Market pressure action plan:

1. **Read the sustainability report.** Every major tech company publishes one. Find the data on water use, electricity consumption, and emissions. Use those numbers at public hearings.

2. **Contact your pension fund.** State pension funds are among the largest holders of Big Tech shares. Ask the fund's investment committee how it votes on climate and environmental proposals.

3. **Support employee organizing.** Amazon Employees for Climate Justice and similar groups work from inside. If you know people at tech companies, share what is happening in your community.

4. **Connect with organizations that fight for free.** Earthjustice, the Southern Environmental Law Center, and the NAACP have filed data center pollution cases at no cost to the affected communities. If your community already carries a heavy pollution burden, these groups may take your case.

5. **Write to the company.** A letter from an individual does not change a corporation. But a letter from a coalition, a pension fund, or an elected official gets read. Combine market pressure with government action for the strongest result.

CHAPTER NINE

Fight Together

In Prince George's County, Maryland, more than 22,500 people signed a petition opposing data center development. The county executive signed an executive order pausing all data center permits. The county council passed a 180-day moratorium. A task force established months earlier delivered its recommendations by November.

Those signatures did not appear overnight. Someone organized that petition. Someone collected those names. Someone made sure thousands of people knew what was happening and cared enough to act.

Here is how to do that.

Community organizing is the engine behind every successful fight in this book. Moratoria do not pass themselves. Public records requests do not file themselves. Planning boards do not change course because one person sends an email.

People make it happen. Organized people make it happen faster.

9.1 Start With Five People

You do not need a thousand volunteers. You need five people who will show up every time.

Find them among your neighbors, your church, your PTA, your local environmental group. Look for people who are affected by the project—they live near the site, or their water comes from the same source, or their electric bill just went up.

Before the first group meeting, talk to people one at a time. Knock on doors. Have a five-minute conversation: what have you heard, what worries you, would you come to a meeting? A face-to-face conversation at someone's front door is worth more than a hundred social media posts.

You are not recruiting supporters. You are finding leaders—people who will take on tasks and bring others.

Hold a first meeting. It can be at someone's kitchen table. Bring a copy of the permit application, the developer's proposal, and a printed map of the site. Assign tasks: one person requests public records, one person reads the zoning code, one person finds the next hearing date, one person starts a contact list.

In Peculiar, Missouri, a group called "Don't Dump Data on Peculiar" started with a handful of neighbors. Within months, they had convinced the Board of Aldermen to exclude data centers from the zoning code entirely.

In Hancock County, Indiana, residents packed a single public meeting. Their testimony was so critical that the developer withdrew its rezoning application.

You do not need an army. You need a squad.

Give the group a name. It does not need to be clever. "Citizens Against the Data Center" works. "Protect Our Water" works. A name gives the group an identity that reporters can cite, officials can address, and neighbors can join.

Register a social media account the same day. Create a shared email list or group text—when the hearing date is announced, you need to reach everyone within hours. The name makes the effort real.

9.2 Educate Before You Organize

Most people in your community have never heard of a conditional use permit or a rate case. Before you ask them to act, help them understand what is happening.

9.2.1 The Community Meeting

Host a public meeting within the first two weeks. Pick a venue that holds at least 50 people—a library, a church hall, a fire station.

Structure it simply. Spend 20 minutes explaining the project: what it is, who is behind it, what it will do to the community. Spend 10 minutes on what the community can do: attend the hearing, file comments, request records. Spend 30 minutes on questions.

Do not invite the developer. This is your meeting, for your community. The developer will run its own public presentations with professional staff and prepared materials. You are leveling the field.

If you cannot get 50 people in the room, do not worry. Start with what you have. The community meeting in Culpeper, Virginia, that led to a unanimous planning commission denial of a $12 billion project did not start with thousands of supporters. It started with people who cared about their neighborhood showing up to explain why.

9.2.2 What to Cover

Keep the meeting focused on facts, not emotions. Explain what the developer wants to build: square footage, power demand, water use. Explain what the community gives up: tax revenue, water, quiet, open space. Explain what the community can do: file comments, attend the hearing, contact their representative.

End with a sign-up sheet. Get names, email addresses, and phone numbers. Ask each person to commit to one task: attend the next hearing, write a comment, share the fact sheet with five neighbors.

Specificity matters. A meeting that ends with "we should do something" produces nothing. A meeting that ends with "Jane will file the FOIA request by Friday and Mike will draft comments for the planning board by next Tuesday" produces action.

FOIA request   A request under the Freedom of Information Act—a law that gives you the right to ask the government for copies of its documents, emails, and records. Most states have their own version. The government usually must respond within days or weeks.

9.2.3 The One-Page Fact Sheet

Write a single page that explains the project in plain language. Include: the developer's name, the project size, the projected water and electricity use, the tax breaks offered, and the date of the next public hearing.

Print 200 copies. Hand them out at the grocery store, the post office, the high school football game. Tape one to the bulletin board at the library.

People will not read a 50-page planning report. They will read one page if you hand it to them.

The best fact sheets use comparisons. Instead of "1.5 million gallons per day," write "enough water to supply 15,000 homes." Instead of "65 decibels at the property line," write "as loud as a running dishwasher, 24 hours a day, every day." Instead of "$80 million in tax breaks over 20 years," write "enough to hire 500 teachers for a decade."

Numbers in context are harder to ignore than numbers in isolation.

The fact sheet should answer five questions: What is being proposed? What will it cost the community? What are the risks? When is the next hearing? What can people do right now?

If the reader knows those answers, they are ready to act.

Post it on social media. Email it to your neighborhood listserv. Leave copies at the coffee shop, the barbershop, the library. The goal is saturation: every resident who might be affected should see the fact sheet before the next hearing.

Post the fact sheet on a simple website or social media page for your group. When a reporter searches for data center opposition in your area, your group should appear. A website also creates a searchable record for future residents who face the same developer.

9.3   BUILD THE COALITION

A neighborhood group can attend a hearing. A coalition can change a policy.

9.3.1   *Who to Bring In*

Environmental groups. The Sierra Club, the Audubon Society, local watershed groups. They bring expertise on water, air quality, and wildlife. They also bring mailing lists and media contacts.

Farm organizations. If the project affects farmland, the local Farm Bureau or land conservation group is a natural ally. The Maryland farmers who fought the Piedmont Reliability Project organized through existing agricultural networks.

Ratepayer advocates. If the project will raise electric bills, connect with AARP chapters, consumer groups, or your state's public utility consumer advocate.

Faith communities. Churches, synagogues, and mosques have meeting space, moral authority, and organized congregations. Faith in Place was among the signers of the Sierra Club's open letter to Big Tech CEOs. Pope Leo XIV—the first pope with a mathematics degree—named artificial intelligence as one of the defining challenges of his papacy within days of his election in May 2025. When a pope with a math degree says the physical infrastructure behind AI deserves moral scrutiny, that gives faith leaders in your community solid ground to stand on.

Business owners. Local business owners care about water, noise, and property values. A letter from the chamber of commerce carries weight with elected officials. A restaurant owner who says "my customers are complaining about the noise" is harder to dismiss than a resident making the same complaint.

Historic preservation groups. If the project threatens a historic site, battlefield, or cultural landmark, preservation groups bring legal tools and public sympathy.

When you approach a potential partner, call—do not email. Explain how the data center affects their specific concern: water for the farm bureau, noise for the neighborhood association, tax revenue for the school board. Bring your one-page fact sheet. Ask what they need, not just what you need.

In Virginia, the Data Center Reform Coalition grew to more than 50 organizations—environmental groups, homeowner associations, historic preservation societies, and civic organizations. No single group could have achieved that reach. The coalition organized a Data Center Reform Lobby Day in Richmond, bringing members from across the state to meet with legislators on the same day. That kind of coordinated action gets attention.

Organizations that litigate for free. Earthjustice, the Southern Environmental Law Center, the NAACP, the Institute for Justice, and Fair Shake Environmental Legal Services take data center cases at no cost to communities. If your community faces pollution, property condemnation, or government overreach, contact them early. See Appendix C for contact information.

9.3.2 *What Holds Coalitions Together*

Coalitions fall apart when members disagree about the goal. Some want to stop the project. Others want to negotiate better terms. Both positions are valid.

Agree on a common set of demands, not a single outcome. For example: "We demand a public hearing, a noise study, a water impact study, and a community benefit agreement." That list unites both camps. People who want to stop the project get the studies—which may reveal deal-breaking problems. People who want better terms get the CBA as a negotiating tool.

Before you start, map the power. Write down every person who will vote on this project: planning board members, county supervisors, the mayor. For each one, ask: who do they listen to? Who funds their campaigns? What do they care about?

Look up campaign contributions on your state's election commission website or OpenSecrets.org. Check who appointed the planning board members. Read the local newspaper's coverage of the officials involved. Ask neighbors who know local politics: who does this board member listen to? Every community has these networks—you need to learn them.

Hold regular meetings—every two weeks at minimum during active phases. Share information. Celebrate small wins. A coalition is not a one-time event. It is a campaign.

9.3.3 *Keep It Bipartisan*

Data center opposition does not follow party lines. Senator Bernie Sanders proposed a national moratorium. Governor Ron DeSantis proposed banning utility cost pass-throughs and giving local governments the power to reject data centers. Republican state lawmakers in at least six states have backed or introduced moratorium or restriction bills, sometimes breaking with their own party's federal leadership.

Among public officials who have opposed data center projects, roughly 55% are Republican and 45% are Democrat. A Virginia organizer put it simply: "Regardless of whether you're a Republican or a Democrat, you just don't want it."

That unity is your greatest asset. Protect it.

Lead with local impact, not ideology. The messages that hold coalitions together are about bills, water, noise, and property values—not about climate policy or corporate greed. In Coweta County, Georgia, a conservative community, organizers avoided carbon footprint arguments entirely. "Talking about the carbon footprint is just not going to sway anybody in Coweta County," one leader said. The Prince William County coalition leader was blunt: "Whatever feelings you all might have about whatever other issue cannot get in the way of the threat we are facing."

Avoid partisan labels. Do not frame this as a Republican or Democratic issue. Do not attach your data center fight to national political debates. If a reporter asks whether this is a left-wing or right-wing cause, the answer is: "It is a community issue."

Welcome everyone who shows up. A Republican county supervisor and a Sierra Club volunteer may disagree about everything else. On data centers, they are allies. Let them be.

9.3.4 Money

You will need some money, but not much. Printing fact sheets, renting a meeting room, filing FOIA requests, and running a website costs a few hundred dollars. A legal challenge costs more—see Chapter 6 for how to manage legal costs.

Pass the hat at the first community meeting. Set up a small fund. Keep the accounting transparent—nothing undermines a coalition faster than questions about money.

If your group plans to lobby elected officials, consider forming a 501(c)(4) nonprofit—this lets you lobby without limits on spending. Talk to a nonprofit attorney before filing; most charge a flat fee for the paperwork. Many successful groups never formalize. A shared email, a document folder, and a checking account are enough to start.

9.3.5 Dealing with the Developer

If you meet the developer, do it on your terms—your turf, your time, your moderator. Bring your list of conditions from Chapter 7. Record the meeting. Insist on written answers—a verbal promise is worth nothing. Do not negotiate alone.

9.3.6 Choose a Spokesperson

Pick someone who stays calm under pressure and can deliver your message in 60 seconds. The best spokesperson is not always the angriest person in the room—it is the person the local paper will quote accurately. If different coalition members give contradictory quotes, the story becomes about the disagreement, not the project.

9.4 Use the Press

Media coverage changes the power balance. A developer negotiating in private has all the power. A developer negotiating in the newspaper shares it.

Press releases. When you file a records request, submit comments, or pack a hearing—issue a press release. One paragraph on what happened and why it matters. One paragraph with a quote from a named resident. One paragraph of background. Contact information at the bottom. Email it to the reporter who covers local government, the TV station, and any regional outlet.

Social media. A video of 200 people at a hearing, posted the same night, reaches more people than a newspaper story two days later. Record the hearing. Post the key moments. Tag the developer, officials, and the news station. The No Desert Data Center Coalition in Arizona connected with groups nationally through social media and shared tactics across campaigns.

Letters to the editor. Under 300 words. Cite a specific number—gallons of water, decibels of noise, millions in tax breaks. Name the officials who will decide. A letter creates a permanent record that reporters and researchers will find.

Petitions. In 2025, at least 113 petitions on Change.org gathered about 50,000 total signatures. Petitions work best with a specific demand: not "stop the data center" but "hold a public hearing before approving the rezoning." Combine online and in-person collection—a clipboard at the farmers' market reaches people who do not use the internet.

National media. NPR, Fortune, Heatmap News, and Fast Company have all covered data center opposition as a national story. If your story has a strong angle like water scarcity, health impacts, or a secret NDA, pitch it to national outlets. National coverage gives your local fight credibility and makes officials nervous.

9.4.1 The Message That Works

The most effective message crosses party lines. It is not about technology. It is about fairness.

"Your electric bill went up so a data center could get a discount. That is not fair."

Other messages that have worked:

- "They signed an NDA so you could not find out what they promised."
- "One billion gallons of water for a building with 50 employees."
- "The tax break costs more than the school budget."

Keep the message short. Repeat it at every hearing, in every press release, on every fact sheet.

9.5 ELECTIONS

Every tool in this book works better when the right people hold office. Find out when your planning board seats are up for election. In most communities, these races draw fewer than 2,000 voters. A dozen volunteers knocking doors can change the outcome.

9.5.1 The Races That Matter

Local. Planning board members, county supervisors, and city council members decide whether data centers get built. A motivated group of 200 residents can swing the outcome.

In Warrenton, Virginia, residents organized for four years and eventually replaced the council that approved the project—the full story is in Chapter 10.

State. In 2025, Democrat John McAuliff won a Virginia state delegate seat by running almost entirely on data center opposition. He flipped a deep-red district that had not elected a Democrat in more than three decades. In Texas, Republican Rena Schroeder made data center opposition the centerpiece of her state senate campaign. Data center opposition is bipartisan—see Chapter 1. Republicans win on tax giveaways and grid strain. Democrats win on environmental impacts and water.

Utility commissions. Ten states elect their utility commissioners. A group with a clear message can win these quiet races: who should pay for data center grid upgrades?

Identify candidates for the next local and state elections. If no one is running on this issue, recruit someone or run yourself. Ask at your coalition meeting: who has the credibility, the time, and the stomach for a campaign? A candidate who lives near the site and can say "I drink this water" is hard to beat in a low-turnout race.

9.5.2 *The Voter Guide*

Before the next election, create a voter guide. List every candidate for local and state office. Ask each one: where do you stand on data center tax breaks, water use, and ratepayer protection? Publish their answers on social media, at community meetings, and at the polls.

A voter guide tells voters who supports their position. More important, it tells candidates that the issue has an organized constituency. In Virginia, a coalition voter guide reached tens of thousands of voters before the 2025 elections. Candidates who had never mentioned data centers suddenly had positions on them.

9.6 KEEP GOING

The hardest part of community organizing is sustaining it. The first hearing draws 200 people. The sixth hearing draws 20. The developer is counting on you to get tired.

Think of your campaign as a ladder. Each step raises the pressure: first a letter, then a petition, then a packed hearing, then a recall threat, then a lawsuit. You do not start with a lawsuit. You start with the cheapest, easiest action and escalate only when the previous step does not work. Each step shows the decision-maker that ignoring you costs more than listening.

9.6.1   Pace Yourself

Set realistic expectations. The fight may take months or years—Warrenton took four. Do not measure success by whether you stop the first project. Measure it by whether the next project faces a harder path. A moratorium, a zoning change, or a noise ordinance protects the community against every future application.

Rotate tasks among members—one person on the rate case, one on the zoning code, one on the water permit. Burnout kills campaigns faster than the developer does.

9.6.2   When You Lose

Not every fight ends in victory (see the Bessemer case study in Chapter 10). That is worth saying plainly, because nobody else will.

Losing is exhausting. Months of meetings, hearings, and phone calls—and the project gets approved anyway. People blame each other. Marriages feel the strain. The temptation is to walk away and never look at a zoning code again.

If the developer threatens to sue you for speaking out, know that most states have anti-SLAPP laws that protect public hearing testimony and advocacy. SLAPP stands for Strategic Lawsuit Against Public Participation. If you receive a legal threat, contact an attorney immediately—but do not let the threat silence you. Public comments at government hearings are protected speech in every state.

A loss still creates a record. The NDA problem, the jobs question, the transparency demand—all of it is now on the public record. The next community that faces the same developer starts with that knowledge.

If you lose, write down what happened while it is fresh: what worked, what did not, what you wish you had known. Share it with national organizations—Data Center Watch, Kairos Fellowship, your state press association.

Then take a break. You earned it. The fight is not over, but it does not need to consume every evening.

Guard against burnout. The developer has paid staff. You have volunteers with jobs and families. Set boundaries, hold meetings on a regular schedule, and let people take breaks without guilt. A group of ten that lasts two years is more effective than a group of fifty that burns out in three months.

9.6.3 Celebrate Wins

Every moratorium is a win. Every public hearing where residents outnumber the developer's consultants is a win. Every public records request that reveals a secret NDA is a win. Every election where a candidate runs on your issue is a win.

These wins add up. In the second quarter of 2025 alone, data center opponents blocked or delayed projects worth more than $98 billion. That number exists because communities organized.

Track your wins in writing. A shared document that lists every hearing attended, every comment filed, every moratorium won, and every press story published keeps the group motivated. It also provides a record for the next campaign. When a new developer arrives, you can show the planning board exactly what the community has already accomplished.

9.6.4 Find National Allies

You do not have to build everything from scratch. Kairos Fellowship offers trainings and organizing support for communities fighting data centers, and is launching a dedicated data center hotline. Data Center Watch publishes reports tracking opposition campaigns across the country. The Sierra Club, Earthjustice, and the Southern Environmental Law Center provide legal support. See Appendix C for a full list of organizations and contact information.

At least 188 groups nationwide are now organized against data center development (see Chapter 10). Start with an email. Describe the situation in your community and what you need. The knowledge these groups have built is available to you: what works, which lawyers to call, which arguments resonate.

Document your fight for the next community. Share your moratorium ordinance, public records requests, and hearing testimony. Send your story to Data Center Watch. The next community that faces a data center proposal will search for examples—make sure yours is available.

9.7 AFTER THE APPROVAL: KEEP WATCHING

The permit was approved. The data center got built. The fight is not over. Conditions only work if somebody checks whether they are being met.

9.7.1 Organize a Monitoring Network

Divide the work among neighbors. Two people alternate noise monitoring weeks. One person documents light from the property line. One watches drainage ditches after storms. Well water users test quarterly on the same schedule so results can be compared.

Collect all entries in a shared folder or spreadsheet. Multiple independent records from different households are harder to dismiss than one complaint from one address. When three neighbors log the same noise spike on the same Tuesday night, the pattern speaks for itself. See Chapter 6 for documentation protocols—noise measurements, water testing, air quality monitoring. See Appendix B for observation log templates.

> **Monthly Entries Beat Annual Summaries**
>
> A log showing the noise ordinance was exceeded on 23 of 30 days is more persuasive at an enforcement hearing than "noise was frequently too loud." The pattern is the evidence.

9.7.2 When Conditions Are Violated

File code enforcement complaints in writing—not by phone. You need a time-stamped record that you reported the violation and that the government received it.

If you get no response within 30 days, escalate to your state environmental agency. The state agency that issued the air or water permit enforces those conditions. For conditions attached to the local approval, go to the body that approved the project.

Keep copies of every complaint you file and every response you receive. If violations cause property damage, such as cracked foundations from vibration, a well that went dry, or health problems from diesel exhaust, see Chapter 6 for how to find a lawyer.

> ### ☑ What You Can Do
>
> **Organizing action plan:**
>
> 1. **Find five people.** Start with your immediate neighbors. Assign tasks at the first meeting: records requests, zoning research, hearing dates, contact list.
>
> 2. **Host a public meeting and build a coalition.** Within two weeks, explain the project and hand out a one-page fact sheet. Bring in environmental groups, farm organizations, ratepayer advocates, and local businesses.
>
> 3. **Use the press.** Issue press releases. Start a petition with a specific demand. Pitch the story to local and national media.
>
> 4. **Plan for elections.** Identify candidates who will fight for your community. If none exist, recruit one or run yourself. Local races are small enough to win.
>
> 5. **Keep watching after approval.** Organize a monitoring network among neighbors. Divide tasks: noise, light, water, stormwater. File violations in writing.

CHAPTER TEN

Fight on Every Front

Between May 2024 and June 2025, community opposition contributed to blocking or delaying more than $160 billion in data center projects—measured by announced investment value. Not every cancellation was caused by opposition alone. Some developers walked away for financial reasons or because they could not secure power. But organized resistance was a factor in each case.

The pace accelerated: $64 billion through March, then $98 billion in the following quarter alone. Twenty-five projects were canceled outright. Twenty-one of those cancellations came in the second half of 2025.

Opposition grew 125% from the first quarter of 2025 to the second. By the end of the year, more than 230 organizations had signed a letter to Congress calling for a national moratorium.

None of that happened because one community filed one complaint. It happened because communities used every tool in this book—at the same time.

What made the difference? They fought on more than one front at the same time—local, state, and federal. The case studies below show how, and what you can do today.

10.1 The Multi-Front Campaign

The most effective communities do not pick one tool. They use all of them.

Start with a moratorium to buy time. File public records requests to reveal what the developer has been doing in private. Testify at the planning hearing so your concerns go on the official record. Meanwhile, a rate case filing at the utility commission protects your electric bill.

If the noise or light crosses your property line, a nuisance claim gives you standing in court. Shareholder proposals and press stories put pressure on the company and the officials. And when the officials still will not listen, elections replace them.

No single tool wins the fight. The combination does.

10.1.1 Why Multi-Front Campaigns Work

The developer's advantage is resources. Your advantage is that a community fighting on five fronts forces the developer to defend on five fronts. That is expensive, distracting, and risky.

A multi-front campaign also creates multiple paths to success. If the zoning challenge fails, the rate case may succeed. If the rate case fails, the election may change the officials who make the next decision. You do not need to win every battle. You need to win one.

10.1.2 How It Works in Practice

Here is what a multi-front campaign looks like, week by week.

Week 1. Find five people. File a public records request for all NDAs, developer correspondence, tax abatement terms, and economic impact studies. Read the zoning code. Identify the next hearing date.

Week 2. Host a community meeting. Hand out fact sheets. Start a petition with a specific demand—not "stop the data center" but "hold a public hearing before approving the rezoning." Contact the local newspaper. Issue a press release announcing the petition and the community meeting.

Week 3. Submit written comments to the planning board. Ask the board to move data centers from by-right to conditional use. Ask for a moratorium. Call your state representative and ask where they stand on data center tax breaks.

Month 2. Attend the hearing. Bring 20 people. Focus testimony on noise, water, tax breaks, and jobs. File comments with the state utility commission on any pending rate case.

Month 3. Build the coalition. Bring in environmental groups, farm organizations, and ratepayer advocates. If the developer has violated air or water permits, report it to the EPA regional office and the state environmental agency.

If the project site has wetlands, check whether a Section 404 permit has been filed.

Month 4. Review the public records you requested. Build a timeline of who knew what and when. If the records reveal NDAs, secret meetings, or undisclosed terms, issue a press release. Share the findings with your coalition and with the press.

Month 6. Evaluate the results. If the project was approved with weak conditions, consider legal action. If the next election is within a year, start recruiting candidates. If the state legislature is in session, push for tax break reform and water disclosure requirements. Contact your state's attorney general and consumer advocate about ratepayer impacts.

After Month 6. Shift to the long game. If the project was approved, focus on monitoring and enforcement (Chapter 6, Chapter 7). If elections are approaching, recruit candidates or run yourself (Chapter 9). If state legislation is pending, coordinate testimony with allied groups.

The multi-front campaign is not a checklist you follow once. It is a cycle you repeat. Each time through, you have more information, more allies, and more experience.

The first hearing is the hardest. By the sixth, you know the process, the players, and the arguments.

10.2 COMMUNITIES THAT DID IT

10.2.1 Warrenton, Virginia: Four Years to a Ban

Warrenton is a small town in Fauquier County, Virginia, with a population of about 10,000. In 2021, the town council approved zoning that cleared the way for Amazon to build a 220,000-square-foot data center.

Residents organized. Over the next four years, more than 2,300 people wrote letters or spoke at hearings. They pushed for stricter zoning. They showed up meeting after meeting. They built a case that a data center did not belong in a small town.

They did not just testify. They tracked every vote. They identified which council members supported the project and which opposed it. They recruited candidates to run against the supporters.

In 2025, they replaced the council members who had approved the project—some were voted out, others chose not to run. Five new members, all elected on anti-data-center platforms, took office. In July 2025, the new council voted 6–0 to repeal data center zoning entirely. Five incoming council members declared that "no data center has any place in a small town like Warrenton."

The tools: public testimony, coalition building, sustained pressure, and elections. The timeline: four years. The lesson: persistence matters more than any single hearing.

10.2.2 *Prince William County, Virginia: Litigation and Beyond*

The Prince William Digital Gateway would have been the largest data center campus in the world—2,100 acres, 23 million square feet. The county approved the rezoning in December 2023 after a 27-hour public hearing.

Eleven residents and a homeowners association sued. They argued the public notice was defective. The court agreed and voided the rezoning.

The developers appealed. The county allocated $400,000 to defend its decision in court. Construction is barred while the appeal is pending.

But the lawsuit was not the only tool. Residents also filed comments during the rezoning process, organized community groups, and worked with the Coalition to Protect Prince William County. They connected their fight to broader state-level reform efforts.

The tools: litigation, public testimony, coalition building, and state-level advocacy. The timeline: ongoing since 2023. The lesson: a procedural challenge stopped a $25 billion project because the public notice was defective. Forget novel legal theories. Read the rules and find where the developer cut corners.

10.2.3 *Peculiar, Missouri: Zoning Before the Project*

The town of Peculiar, Missouri, did not wait for a problem. When Diode Ventures proposed a $1.5 billion data center, residents formed a group called "Don't Dump Data on Peculiar." They organized around noise, visual impact, and property values.

By October 2024, the Board of Aldermen had amended the zoning code to exclude data centers entirely.

The tools: grassroots organizing, local government engagement, and a zoning change. The timeline: months, not years.

10.2.4 Bessemer, Alabama: When the Fight Does Not Win

Not every fight ends in victory. In Bessemer, a developer proposed a 4.5-million-square-foot data center needing 1,200 megawatts—enough for 760,000 homes. Residents, the NAACP, and the SELC opposed the project.

City officials had signed NDAs. NDAs blocked the basic facts about the deal. No public records request could pierce them. Residents fought blind, unable to challenge terms they were not allowed to see.

The council voted to approve data centers in light industrial areas. The project went through.

But the fight was not wasted. It put the NDA problem on the public record, brought the NAACP into data center opposition, and showed other Alabama communities what to watch for. Every fight creates a record. A loss in one community is a tool for the next.

10.2.5 Prince George's County, Maryland: Petitions to Policy

Prince George's County (see Chapter 9) showed that petitions translate to policy: signatures led to a moratorium, a task force, and permanent zoning rules within months. When enough people act, the political system responds fast.

10.2.6 Arizona: Tract and the Revised Approach

In 2024, Tract proposed a $14 billion data center campus near Buckeye, Arizona. Residents organized around building heights, noise, and utility strain. Tract withdrew the application. By August, the company announced a revised project on a site away from residential neighborhoods.

Community pressure does not always kill a project. Sometimes it reshapes one. A project that moves away from homes, reduces its water draw, or adds noise limits is a better outcome than an uncontested approval. The families who no longer live next to a cooling tower know.

10.3   THE LONG GAME

Some fights end in months. Others take years. The most important ones change the rules so the next community does not have to fight as hard.

The movement is growing fast, and it is broadening. Communities that organized around a data center are discovering that the same fight applies to the transmission lines, solar farms, and battery storage facilities the project demands. At least 188 activist groups nationwide are now organized against data center development. Of 25 data center projects canceled due to local opposition in 2025, 21 were canceled in the second half of the year.

Other communities have already built the playbook. You are joining a national movement that is already winning.

10.3.1   *What the Movement Has Won*

Communities in at least 24 states have enacted data center moratoria. Michigan alone has 26. Loudoun County ended by-right data center construction.

Illinois proposed freezing its incentive program. Virginia created a new rate class that requires data centers to pay for their own capacity. Candidates have won elections on this issue in Virginia, New Jersey, and Georgia.

None of this existed five years ago. Five states have introduced bills to ban NDAs between developers and local officials. The infrastructure for this fight exists. Use it.

The national organizations supporting this work are listed in Appendix C: Kairos Fellowship, Data Center Watch, Food & Water Watch, the Sierra Club, Earthjustice, and the SELC.

10.3.2   *What Happens After You Win*

A moratorium expires. A denied rezoning can be refiled. Winning a single fight is not the end—the goal is to change the rules so the next fight is easier.

After a moratorium, adopt permanent regulations: setbacks, noise limits, conditional use requirements. A moratorium without follow-up is a delay, not a solution.

Build institutional memory. Save every document—the rezoning application, the public records responses, the hearing transcripts. After you defeat a rezoning, watch for the developer to come back with a revised plan. For permanent zoning protections, see the conditions list in Chapter 3. For enforceable agreements with developers, see the CBA checklist in Chapter 7.

After you win an election, hold the new officials accountable. Track the votes. If the new council member does not follow through, remind them publicly of their campaign promises.

The developer's advantage is patience—lawyers on retainer, lobbyists on salary. Your advantage is that you live there. You are not leaving.

10.3.3 Change the Zoning Code

After a moratorium expires, adopt permanent rules (Chapter 3). PennFuture's model data center ordinance provides ready-to-adopt language for setbacks, noise limits, and conditional use requirements. York County, Pennsylvania, built its data center zoning from that model. You do not have to draft a zoning amendment from scratch.

10.3.4 Build the Network

If your state has a statewide coalition, join it. If it does not, start one—a shared mailing list and a monthly call are enough. The Virginia Data Center Reform Coalition grew to more than 50 organizations from a handful of groups that were already fighting separate battles.

See Chapter 9 and Appendix C for national organizations that can connect you with experienced organizers. The first email is the hardest. After that, you are part of a network that stretches across more than 20 states.

10.3.5 Change the State Law

Push your state lawmakers on the priorities in Chapter 4: tax reform, water disclosure, ratepayer protection, NDA bans, and environmental review. Since 2024, Illinois froze new data center tax incentives while studying their costs. Five states introduced bills banning NDAs between developers and local officials. Three governors vetoed water disclosure requirements—ask yours why. If your state has not acted on any of these, call your legislator and ask what they are waiting for.

10.3.6 Run for Office

Candidates have won on data center issues at every level, from state delegate to governor, in both parties.

If no one in your area is running on this issue, recruit someone or run yourself. Local races draw fewer than 2,000 votes—a motivated group of 200 can change the outcome.

Your state or county election office lists filing deadlines and requirements. The minimum for most local offices: a filing fee (often under $100), a petition with a small number of signatures, and the willingness to knock on doors. Start with your county party committee or a candidate-recruitment organization.

Do not overlook school board races. School boards control PILOT agreements and how to spend PILOT revenue. A school board that demands transparency on data center payments holds the developer accountable long after the zoning fight is over.

10.4 What You Can Do Today

You now have tools for every level of government, for the courtroom, for the negotiating table, for the boardroom, and for the ballot box.

None of them work if you do not use them.

Here is what you can do today, right now, before you put this book down:

1. Find the project. Search your county planning department website for data center applications. If you do not find one, search for recent rezoning approvals in industrial zones. Check whether your state economic development agency has announced any data center incentive deals.

2. Read the zoning code. Look up whether data centers are permitted by right in any zone in your community. If yes, push for a zoning text amendment.

3. Find the hearing. If a project is proposed, find the next public hearing date. Write it down. Tell five people.

4. File a request. Submit a public records request for any NDAs between your local government and data center developers.

5. Make a call. Call your state representative. Ask where they stand on data center tax breaks, water disclosure, and ratepayer protection.

6. Connect with others. Search online for data center opposition groups in your state. Check the Data Center Watch website for a list of active campaigns. Contact Kairos Fellowship's data center hotline. You do not have to figure this out alone. Somebody in another state has already fought the same fight and can tell you what worked.

Six actions. None takes more than an hour. Together, they start a fight.

10.5 THIS IS NOT OVER

The data center industry spent $320 billion on capital expenditures in 2025 and tens of millions more on lobbying and public relations. The Data Center Coalition nearly tripled its quarterly lobbying spending. Meta is running TV ads about small-town values. The PR budget tells you how worried they are.

Every data center needs land, water, electricity, and a permit. Every permit requires a government decision. Every government decision is subject to public input, legal challenge, and electoral accountability. At every stage, ask the question this book keeps coming back to: *if the optimistic projection is wrong, who bears the downside risk?* If the answer is "you," the deal is not good enough.

Every community that fights a data center makes the next fight easier. Warrenton's ban is a precedent. Prince George's County's moratorium is a model. Michigan's ratepayer protections are a template. Every hearing, every comment, every election adds to a body of knowledge that the next community can use.

> **☑ What You Can Do**
>
> **The complete action plan:**
>
> 1. **Local (Chapter 3).** Check the zoning code. Push for conditional use permits and a moratorium. Attend hearings. File public records requests.
> 2. **State (Chapter 4).** File comments in utility rate cases. Push for tax break reform, water disclosure, and ratepayer protection. Contact your state lawmakers.
> 3. **Federal (Chapter 5).** Check for wetlands and 404 permits. File FERC comments. Ask about air permits. Call your member of Congress.
> 4. **Property and negotiation (Chapter 6, Chapter 7).** Document noise, light, water, and property values. Demand a community benefit agreement with direct payments, water caps, and decommissioning bonds.
> 5. **Together (Chapter 9, Chapter 8).** Find five people. Build a coalition. Use the press. Contact your pension fund. Plan for elections. Keep going.

Appendix A: Glossary

These definitions use plain language. Legal and technical terms have specific meanings that vary by state. When precision matters, consult a lawyer or your state's statutes.

404 permit
A permit required under Section 404 of the Clean Water Act before any-one can fill or disturb wetlands. Issued by the Army Corps of Engineers. Requires public notice and a comment period.

Abatement (tax)
A reduction or elimination of property, sales, or other taxes for a set number of years. Data center abatements can last 10 to 50 years. See also: PILOT.

Behind-the-meter
A power source connected directly to a facility, bypassing the public grid. Does not go through the utility or the interconnection queue.

By-right use
A land use automatically permitted under the zoning code. If data centers are by-right in industrial zones, the developer does not need a public hearing or special approval.

Capacity auction
An auction run by a regional grid operator (like PJM) where power plants bid to be available in future years. Higher demand raises auction prices, which flow through to household electric bills.

Chain of custody
The documented record showing who collected a piece of evidence, who

handled it, and how it was stored. Without chain of custody, a water sample or noise recording can be challenged as altered or contaminated.

Clawback

A provision that lets a community take back tax breaks if the developer does not deliver what it promised—usually a certain number of jobs or level of investment.

Community benefit agreement (CBA)

A contract between a developer and the community. The developer commits to specific benefits—cash payments, jobs, environmental protections—in exchange for community support or approval.

Conditional use permit

Special permission required to build something not normally allowed in a zoning district. Requires a public hearing. The governing body can attach conditions or deny the application. Also called a special use permit or special exception.

Consumer advocate

A state office that represents utility customers in proceedings before the public utility commission. Also called public counsel, people's counsel, or ratepayer advocate.

Decibel (dB)

A unit measuring sound intensity. Normal conversation is about 60 dB. Data center cooling equipment produces 55 to 85 dB. Backup generators can reach 100 to 110 dB.

dBC (C-weighted decibels)

A sound measurement scale that treats all frequencies equally, unlike dBA which filters low frequencies. Data center hum is low-frequency and may read much louder on dBC than dBA.

Decommissioning bond

Money set aside before construction to pay for removing a facility and restoring the site when the project ends. Common for solar farms and wind turbines. Rare for data centers.

Eminent domain

The government's power to take private land for public use, with compensation. Used for roads, utilities, and transmission lines—including lines built to serve data centers.

Environmental impact statement (EIS)

A detailed analysis of how a proposed project will affect the environment. Required under NEPA for major federal actions. Some states have their own environmental review laws.

FERC

The Federal Energy Regulatory Commission. Regulates interstate transmission lines and wholesale electricity markets. Does not regulate data centers directly but oversees the grid that serves them.

FOIA request

A request for government records under the Freedom of Information Act (federal) or your state's equivalent. Also called a public records request or open records request.

Hyperscaler

A company that builds and operates data centers at massive scale, often measured in gigawatts of power demand. Examples include Amazon (AWS), Microsoft (Azure), Google (Google Cloud), Meta, Oracle, CoreWeave, and xAI.

Interconnection queue

The waiting list to connect a new power source or large customer to the electric grid. Wait times average 5 to 10 years.

Moratorium

A temporary pause on new permits or applications. Gives the community time to study impacts and update regulations. Typical duration: 6 to 12 months.

NEPA

The National Environmental Policy Act. Requires federal agencies to study the environmental effects of major actions before approving them. Does not apply to most private data centers unless federal permits or funding are involved.

New Source Review (NSR)

A Clean Air Act permit required when a new facility or major modification will emit significant air pollution. Data centers with many diesel generators may trigger NSR.

NDA (nondisclosure agreement)

A contract that bars parties from sharing certain information. Developers routinely ask local officials to sign NDAs before revealing project details. NDAs between public entities and private companies are public records in most states.

Nuisance (private)

A legal claim that someone else's use of their property unreasonably interferes with your use of yours. The most common legal tool for neighbors affected by data center noise or light.

PILOT (payment in lieu of taxes)

A negotiated annual payment from a developer to a community, used when property taxes have been abated. Ensures schools, fire departments, and roads receive some funding.

PJM Interconnection

The regional grid operator for 13 states and D.C., serving 65 million people. Manages the transmission grid and runs capacity auctions.

PurpleAir

A network of community-owned air quality sensors that measure fine particulate pollution (PM2.5). Sensors cost about $230 and upload data to a public map.

Power Usage Effectiveness (PUE)

A ratio measuring data center electricity efficiency. A PUE of 1.3 means that for every watt powering servers, another 0.3 watts goes to cooling and overhead.

Prior appropriation

A water rights system used in most western states. The rule is "first in time, first in right." Senior water rights holders get their full share before junior holders get any.

Public utility commission (PUC)

A state agency that regulates electric, gas, and water utilities. Sets the rates your utility can charge. Also called a public service commission (PSC) in some states.

Rate base

The total value of a utility's assets on which it is allowed to earn a return. When a utility builds infrastructure to serve data centers, the cost goes into the rate base and is spread across all customers.

Rate case

A proceeding at the public utility commission where a utility requests permission to change the rates it charges. The public can file comments and testify.

Referendum

A vote by the public on a specific question, such as whether to overturn a zoning decision. Rules vary by state.

Renewable energy certificate (REC)

A paper credit representing one megawatt-hour of electricity from renewable sources. Companies buy RECs to claim their electricity is "green," but the certificate may not correspond to power the company actually uses.

Rezoning

Changing the zoning classification of a piece of land—for example, from agricultural to industrial. Usually requires a public hearing and a vote.

Riparian rights

A water rights system used in most eastern states. Landowners next to a body of water have the right to use it in "reasonable" amounts. If a data center's withdrawals impair your use, you may have a legal claim.

Setback

The required distance between a building and the property line, road, or other boundary. Standard industrial setbacks (50 feet) were not designed for data centers. Communities have required 300 to 1,500 feet.

Shell company

A company created to hide the identity of the real owner. Developers use shell companies and code names ("Project Peanut," "Project Blue") when acquiring land.

Taking

A government action that deprives a property owner of the use or value of their property. If a moratorium eliminates all economic use of the land, it may be challenged as a taking. The Supreme Court has upheld temporary moratoria as valid.

Variance

An exception to the zoning rules granted to a specific property owner. Requires a showing of hardship.

Zoning code

The set of local laws that controls what can be built where. Divides land into zones (residential, commercial, industrial, agricultural) and lists the uses allowed in each.

Zoning text amendment

A change to the zoning code itself—for example, adding a definition of "data center" or moving data centers from by-right to conditional use. Requires a public hearing and a vote.

Appendix B: Sample Documents

These templates are starting points. Adapt them to your situation, your state's laws, and your community's needs. A local attorney can help you sharpen the wording.

B.1   Sample Public Records Request

[Your Name]
[Your Address]
[Date]

[Title of Records Custodian]
[Name of Government Body]
[Address]

Re: Public Records Request Under [Your State's Public Records Law]

Dear Records Custodian:

Under [cite your state's public records statute by name and section number], I request copies of the following records:

1. All nondisclosure agreements between [government body] and any data center developer, technology company, or subsidiary tied to data center projects within [jurisdiction].

2. All correspondence between officials or staff of [government body] and any representative of [developer name, if known, or "any data center developer"] from [start date] to the present. This includes emails, letters, text messages, and meeting notes.

3. All tax abatement deals, tax increment financing deals, or economic incentive deals tied to data center projects.

4. All economic impact studies, fiscal analyses, or cost-benefit analyses tied to data center projects, whether ordered by or sent to [government body].

5. All documents about water use, electricity demand, or environmental impact sent by any data center developer to [government body].

I request these records in digital format (PDF preferred) sent to [your email address].

Under [state statute], you are required to respond within [number] business days. If any records are withheld, please provide a written reason for each withheld document, naming the specific exemption relied upon.

I am willing to pay fair copying costs up to $[amount]. Please let me know before running up costs above that amount.

Sincerely,
[Your Name]
[Phone Number]
[Email]

Tips:

- Cite your state's statute by name (e.g., Virginia Freedom of Information Act, Michigan Freedom of Information Act, California Public Records Act).
- Send the request by email and keep a copy with a timestamp.
- If the government delays or denies your request, contact your state press association or open government hotline. Many offer free help.
- You do not need to explain why you want the records.

B.2 SAMPLE PUBLIC COMMENT LETTER

[Your Name]
[Your Address]
[Date]

[Name of Planning Commission/Board of Supervisors/City Council]
[Address]

Re: [Application Number] — [Project Name or Developer Name]
Conditional Use Permit / Rezoning Application

Dear Members of the [Board/Commission]:

I am a resident of [community] and I am writing about the above application for a data center at [location]. I ask the [Board/Commission] to [deny the application / approve only with the following conditions / delay the decision until further study is done].

[Choose the issues that apply to your situation:]

Noise. The application projects [X] decibels at the property line. My home is [distance] from the proposed site. I ask the Board to require pre-construction noise measurements by a licensed engineer and a noise limit of 55 decibels or lower at the property line at night. The Board should also require post-construction monitoring with penalties for violations.

Water. The proposed facility will use [X] gallons of water per day. [Describe your water source—city supply, private well, shared aquifer.] I ask the Board to require a water impact study, a cap on daily water use, a ban on private wells, and closed-loop cooling.

Tax abatement. The proposed [X]-year, [X]% tax abatement will cost the community an estimated $[amount] in lost revenue. I ask the Board to limit the abatement to [10/15] years and require a payment in lieu of taxes during that period. The agreement should include clawback provisions tied to actual job creation.

Jobs. The developer projects [X] permanent jobs. I ask the Board to require the developer to commit to a specific number of permanent, full-time positions at a minimum wage of $[amount] per hour. The agreement should include clawbacks if targets are not met.

Decommissioning. Data center buildings have a typical lifespan of 20 years. I ask the Board to require a decommissioning bond funded before construction begins. The bond should cover the cost of tearing down the building and restoring the site.

Thank you for considering these comments. I request that this letter be entered into the official record.

Sincerely,
[Your Name]
[Phone Number]
[Email]

Tips:

- Submit written comments before the deadline. They carry the same legal weight as speaking at the meeting.
- Use specific numbers from the application. Vague complaints are less effective than quoting the developer's own figures.
- Keep a copy with a timestamp.
- Work with neighbors so different people cover different issues.

B.3 Sample Moratorium Resolution

This template is drawn from the model moratorium language in this book. Adapt it to your state's legal powers and your community's needs.

RESOLUTION NO. [NUMBER]

A RESOLUTION ESTABLISHING A TEMPORARY MORATORIUM ON DATA CENTER DEVELOPMENT IN [JURISDICTION]

WHEREAS, [Jurisdiction] has received [inquiries from / applications by] data center developers proposing [facilities / campuses] within [Jurisdiction]; and

WHEREAS, the [Zoning Code / Land Use Ordinance] of [Jurisdiction] does not define "data center" or set rules for the unique impacts of data center facilities; and

WHEREAS, data centers present impacts not addressed by existing regulations, including but not limited to: high electricity demand, water consumption for cooling, and noise from mechanical equipment; and

WHEREAS, these impacts also include backup diesel generator emissions, light pollution, and demands on public infrastructure; and

WHEREAS, [Jurisdiction] has not conducted a study of the impacts of data center development on [water supply / electric grid / noise levels / property values / public services]; and

WHEREAS, [cite your state's legal authority for moratoria—police power, home rule authority, or specific moratorium statute]; and

WHEREAS, the [Board/Council] finds that a temporary moratorium is needed to protect the health, safety, and welfare of residents while [Jurisdiction] studies these impacts and writes proper rules;

NOW, THEREFORE, BE IT RESOLVED:

Section 1. Moratorium. A temporary moratorium is hereby placed on the acceptance, review, and approval of applications for new data center facilities within [Jurisdiction]. For purposes of this resolution, "data center" means a building used mainly for storing, managing, or processing digital data, including its power and cooling systems. A facility meets this definition if it covers more than 10,000 square feet of floor area or needs more than 2 megawatts of power.

Section 2. Duration. This moratorium shall stay in effect for [6/12] months from the date of adoption, or until [Jurisdiction] adopts new rules for data center projects, whichever comes first.

Section 3. Exemptions. This moratorium does not apply to:

155

(a) Data center facilities that have received a valid building permit or conditional use permit before the date of this resolution;

(b) Existing data center facilities, including routine upkeep and equipment swaps that do not expand the facility's footprint or power use;

(c) Facilities below the size threshold defined in Section 1.

Section 4. Study. The [Planning Department / designated consultant] shall conduct a study of data center impacts on [Jurisdiction], including water supply, electricity demand, noise, air quality, traffic, property values, and fiscal impact. The study shall include recommendations for zoning rules, permit requirements, and performance standards for data center projects. The study shall be completed and presented to the [Board/Council] within [4/6] months.

Section 5. Effective date. This resolution takes effect right away upon adoption.

Tips:

- The findings (WHEREAS clauses) are the most important part. Strong findings tend to survive legal challenges. Name specific concerns.
- Include exemptions for existing facilities and approved permits. This lowers the risk of a takings challenge.
- Include a study requirement. A moratorium with no study looks like a stall tactic.
- Have your town attorney review the draft before the vote. The attorney should confirm the legal basis cited is correct for your state.

B.4   COMMUNITY BENEFIT AGREEMENT CHECKLIST

Use this checklist when talking terms with a data center developer. Not every item will apply to every project. The goal is to make sure the community gets clear, enforceable benefits.

Direct Payments

☐ Yearly cash payments to the community (not just vague promises of growth)

- ☐ Payment amount scales with the size of the project (e.g., per megawatt or per square foot)
- ☐ Payments indexed to inflation
- ☐ Payments begin before or at the start of construction, not after completion

Jobs

- ☐ Specific number of permanent, full-time positions (not "up to" or "estimated")
- ☐ Minimum wage for permanent staff (e.g., $25/hour or above)
- ☐ Local hiring preference (share of workers from the community)
- ☐ Going wage rate for construction workers
- ☐ Clawback: benefits cut if job targets are missed, checked yearly

Water

- ☐ Hard cap on daily water use (in gallons per day)
- ☐ Closed-loop cooling required (no water-wasting cooling)
- ☐ Ban on private wells; municipal water only
- ☐ Yearly public reports on actual water use
- ☐ Water impact study done before approval

Noise

- ☐ Noise cap at the property line (55 dB or lower at night)
- ☐ Baseline noise readings before construction, taken by a licensed engineer
- ☐ Noise checks after construction (yearly or ongoing)
- ☐ Fines for violations (not just warnings)
- ☐ Generator testing only during the day (e.g., 10 a.m. to 4 p.m.)

Tax Abatement Terms

- ☐ Sunset clause: abatement expires after 10 to 15 years maximum
- ☐ Performance trigger: abatement share tied to actual job creation
- ☐ Payment in lieu of taxes (PILOT) during the abatement period
- ☐ PILOT funds sent to schools, fire departments, and public services
- ☐ Incentive bids posted online 90 days before any approval vote

Transparency

- ☐ No NDA on the agreement itself—all public terms are public
- ☐ True owner named (not just the shell company)
- ☐ Yearly public reports on water use, energy use, noise levels, and jobs
- ☐ Reports checked by an outside party, not the developer

Decommissioning

- ☐ Teardown bond funded before construction begins
- ☐ Bond covers building removal and site cleanup
- ☐ Bond amount reviewed and adjusted every 5 years

Environmental

- ☐ Backup generators meet EPA Tier 4 exhaust standards
- ☐ Setback of at least 300 feet from homes
- ☐ Landscaping buffer around the site edge
- ☐ Full cutoff lighting (no light spillover)
- ☐ Stormwater runoff plan

Ratepayer Protection

- ☐ Developer pays for power grid upgrades the facility causes
- ☐ Long-term power purchase contract (15 years minimum)
- ☐ Minimum billing: developer pays for at least 80% of reserved power
- ☐ Data center load cut before homes during grid emergencies

B.5   OBSERVATION LOG TEMPLATES

Three log formats for community monitoring. Paper or digital—the format matters less than the habit. Fill in every column for every entry. A blank cell is a gap a lawyer will ask about.

B.5.1 General Observation Log

Date	Time	Weather	Loca-tion	Observation	Photo	Ob-server

B.5.2 Well Water Log

Record static water level before pumping and dynamic level after five minutes of pumping.

Date	Static (ft)	Dy-namic (ft)	Flow (gpm)	Appearance	Lab	Notes

B.5.3 Noise Log

Take at least 10 readings per session, spaced two minutes apart. Record the average and peak values.

Date	Time	Weather	Meter	dBA	dBC	Ambi-ent	Loca-tion	Notes

Appendix C: Resources

Websites and contact information may change. Search for the organization name if a link no longer works.

C.1 National Organizations

Food & Water Watch — Research and advocacy on data center water use and jobs; published the national moratorium letter signed by 230+ groups. https://www.foodandwaterwatch.org

Sierra Club — Environmental advocacy with local chapters in every state; active on data center energy campaigns. https://www.sierraclub.org

Earthjustice — Nonprofit environmental law firm; litigates at no cost to clients; 14 regional offices. https://earthjustice.org

Southern Environmental Law Center (SELC) — Free legal representation for environmental cases in the Southeast. https://www.southernenvironmental.org

Good Jobs First — Research on corporate subsidies, tax breaks, and accountability. Use the Subsidy Tracker to search data center tax breaks by state: https://subsidytracker.goodjobsfirst.org

Kairos Fellowship — Connects communities organizing against data centers; offers training and resources. https://www.kairosfellows.org/fightdatacenters

MediaJustice — Research on data center pollution and community health impacts, particularly in the South. https://mediajustice.org

American Farm Bureau Federation — State and county Farm Bureaus advocate for farmland preservation and agricultural land use policy; active on data center farmland conversion. https://www.fb.org

American Farmland Trust — Research on farmland loss, including the "Farms Under Threat" reports documenting agricultural land conversion to data centers and other development. https://farmland.org

Data Center Watch — Tracks community opposition, project cancellations, and organizing efforts. https://www.datacenterwatch.org

NAACP — Environmental and climate justice program; active in data center pollution cases. https://naacp.org

C.2 Legal Resources

Environmental Law Institute — Pro Bono Clearinghouse — Connects communities with volunteer attorneys for environmental legal matters. https://www.eli.org

Fair Shake Environmental Legal Services — Pro bono and sliding-scale legal services in the Mid-Atlantic region. https://www.fairshake-els.org

Institute for Justice — Nonprofit law firm fighting eminent domain abuse and property rights violations at no cost to property owners. https://ij.org

Law School Environmental Clinics — Many law schools take real cases at no cost. Search "environmental law clinic" plus your state to find options near you.

State Bar Referral Services — Every state bar runs a lawyer referral service. Ask for attorneys who handle nuisance, land use, or environmental law.

C.3 Data Sources

Lawrence Berkeley National Laboratory (LBNL) — Most-cited research on U.S. data center energy use. https://eta.lbl.gov

Energy Information Administration (EIA) — Federal data on electricity generation, consumption, and prices by state. https://www.eia.gov

National Wetlands Inventory — Check whether a project site includes wetlands requiring a Section 404 permit. https://www.fws.gov/program/national-wetlands-inventory

EPA ECHO — Search for air and water permit violations by facility. https://echo.epa.gov

OpenSecrets — Tracks lobbying spending and campaign contributions. https://www.opensecrets.org

EPA Drinking Water Lab Locator — Find certified water testing labs by state. https://www.epa.gov/dwlabcert

PurpleAir Map — Community air quality sensor network with real-time PM2.5 data. https://map.purpleair.com

NIOSH Sound Level Meter — Free smartphone app for noise screening, developed by the National Institute for Occupational Safety and Health. Available for iOS and Android.

C.4 GOVERNMENT CONTACTS

Your County or City Planning Office — Project applications, hearing dates, and zoning information. Search "[your county/city] planning department."

Your State Public Utility Commission — Open dockets, public comment portals, and consumer advocate contact information. Search "[your state] public utility commission."

Your State Attorney General — Online complaint forms and consumer protection divisions. Search "[your state] attorney general."

Your State Environmental Agency — Air permits, water permits, and environmental review. Search "[your state] department of environment."

EPA Regional Offices — If your state agency is slow to act on violations, contact the EPA regional office. https://www.epa.gov/aboutepa/regional-and-geographic-offices

Your Members of Congress — Find your representative at https://www.house.gov/representatives/find-your-representative. Find your senators at https://www.senate.gov/senators/senators-contact.htm.

C.5 FURTHER READING

JLARC. *Data Centers in Virginia.* December 2024. Most detailed state-level audit of data center tax incentives.

Good Jobs First. *Cloudy Data, Costly Deals.* November 2025.

Food & Water Watch. *Artificial Jobs.* January 2026. Data center employment claims versus reality.

Brookings Institution. *Why Community Benefit Agreements Are Necessary for Data Centers.* 2025.

Ohio River Valley Institute. *Why Data Centers Will Be Economic Development Duds.* 2025.

Bommarito, Michael James. *Moratorium Nation: A Survey of Data Center, Renewable Energy, and Battery Storage Moratoria in the United States.* February 2026. Survey of 116 moratoria across 30 states with a 13-section model ordinance template. Free at https://ssrn.com/abstract=6242898.

UC Riverside. *AI's Deadly Air Pollution Toll.* December 2024. Health impacts of data center diesel generators.